To Pc. Comp. Howard Pattinson.
We have so many happy fellowship memories!
Long may they continue!
&
May good fellowship go with you always.
Ted Hold,
National Chairman,
2010.

Straight From The Horsa's Mouth

Ted Hold

© Copyright 2006 Edward Hold.
All rights reserved. No part of this publication may be reproduced, stored in a retrieval system, or transmitted, in any form or by any means, electronic, mechanical, photocopying, recording, or otherwise, without the written prior permission of the author.

Note for Librarians: A cataloguing record for this book is available from Library and Archives Canada at www.collectionscanada.ca/amicus/index-e.html
ISBN 1-4251-0538-6

Printed in Victoria, BC, Canada. Printed on paper with minimum 30% recycled fibre. Trafford's print shop runs on "green energy" from solar, wind and other environmentally-friendly power sources.

Offices in Canada, USA, Ireland and UK

Book sales for North America and international:
Trafford Publishing, 6E–2333 Government St.,
Victoria, BC V8T 4P4 CANADA
phone 250 383 6864 (toll-free 1 888 232 4444)
fax 250 383 6804; email to orders@trafford.com

Book sales in Europe:
Trafford Publishing (UK) Limited, 9 Park End Street, 2nd Floor
Oxford, UK OX1 1HH UNITED KINGDOM
phone 44 (0)1865 722 113 (local rate 0845 230 9601)
facsimile 44 (0)1865 722 868; info.uk@trafford.com
Order online at:
trafford.com/06-2296

10 9 8 7 6 5 4 3 2 1

Contents

List of Photographs ii

Acknowledgements iv

Foreword v

Chapter 1   The Seed is Sown 1

Chapter 2   Sunderland P.O. Home Guard 7

Chapter 3   Royal Corps of Signals 14

Chapter 4   The Red Beret 21

Chapter 5   Airborne Initiative 26

Chapter 6   Prelude to D-Day 34

Chapter 7   Destination: Ranville 39

Chapter 8   Entrenched in Ecarde 47

Chapter 9   A Reputation to Uphold 54

Chapter 10 Winter in the Ardennes 58

Chapter 11 Hospitality in Holland 63

Chapter 12 The Rhine Drop 67

Chapter 13 Advance to the Baltic 71

Chapter 14 Victory in Europe 80

Chapter 15 The State of Emergency 89

Chapter 16 Crazy Antics 96

Chapter 17 The Perils of Palestine 100

Chapter 18 Homeward Bound 109

Chapter 19 We'll Meet Again 113

POSTSCRIPT 116

List of Photographs

# 1	The Northumberland Fusiliers Brigade Engineering School Staff in 1919	1
# 2	Edward Hold senior and junior circa 1930	2
# 3	The Home Guard Bombing Course in December 1940	9
# 4	Cross section of a '36' grenade drawn by Ted Hold in December 1940	12
# 5	Raw recruits at the Primary Training Centre Ossett in December 1942	15
# 6	Ena and Ted in Slaithwaite in 1943	19
# 7	Ted wearing the Red Beret and Airborne Flash in September 1943	22
# 8	Invasion currency issued in May 1944	38
# 9	Two Horsas in the fields North of Ranville 10/06/1944	40
# 10	Horsas in the fields near Ranville 15/06/1944	42
# 11	The original Pegasus Bridge still in situ in 1984	50
# 12	The Allied Airborne flash worn (briefly) by members of 6th A/B Div. Sigs	56
# 13	The Chateau de Neffe in 1954	60
# 14	Camille and Emma Devillers	61
# 15	Schoolstraat Panningen	64
# 16	British and American gliders near Hamminkeln 25/03/1945	68
# 17	Rail tickets picked up at Diersfordt station on 24/03/1945	69
# 18	Brewing up in Germany on the way to the Baltic in April 1945	71
# 19	Ted and Wally Petchy at Steinhuder in April 1945	77
# 20	A dead 'Werewolf' outside Wismar Town Hall in May 1945	80
# 21	The Wismar billet	81
# 22	Ted wearing the top hat	81
# 23	Ted, Jim Crotty and Tommy Grant in German uniform	82
# 24	More "High Jinks" at Wismar	82
# 25	Ted enjoying 'Victory in Europe' near Luneburg in May 1945	85
# 26	The Arundel Castle viewed from a barge in Haifa Bay 24/09/1945	90
# 27	On board the Haifa to Deir-el-Balah cattle truck	91
# 28	Ted in khaki drill	94
# 29	The cast of 'Crazy Antics' with Roger Livesey and Ursula Jeans	98
# 30	The H Section football team in October 1945	102
# 31	Ted seeing the funny side of fatigues in December 1945	103
# 32	Ted and 'NANKI-POO' at Nuseirat in November 1945	105
# 33	Ahmed, Ted and Ishmael outside the El Faluja power plant in February 1946	108
# 34	Princess visit to Grindon	114

Acknowledgements

My grateful thanks to my son Anthony for his unstinting work in transcribing my original notes onto computer and preparing them for publication, to my daughter Sheilagh for suggesting the title and to her husband Ken Routledge for helping make this publication a reality.

Photographs 9, 10 and 16 are reproduced by kind permission of the Imperial War Museum and I am indebted to Jim Crotty for the use of photos 18, 22, 23 and 24.

Foreword

It was Anthony who, during the Airborne Pilgrimage to Normandy on the 50th Anniversary of D-Day, suggested that I put all my war reminiscences to paper. He knew that the small contributions I had made to various newspapers and the book "We Remember D-Day" were just the tip of the iceberg and believed that if I did not then a small part of history would, ultimately, be lost. "How many accounts of life in the 6th Airborne have been written from a Signalman's point of view?" he asked. "And besides, you just couldn't make up some of the things that have happened to you." Point taken.

In August 1994 I took my dear wife Ena to Ropner House, a Masonic Convalescent Home in Middleton St. George, and having absolutely nothing to do but relax for a fortnight I started on my memoirs. Looking back I don't think I could have chosen a better time or place, Middleton St. George having been the site of an RAF aerodrome during the war.

As I put my story together over the succeeding months and years, spasmodically and not without prompting, I felt something was missing. War stories weren't enough. I needed a theme, a thread, and when I found it, it was the colour khaki.

What follows is an account of my years in khaki in the Church Lads Brigade, the Home Guard and the Royal Corps of Signals. I hope you enjoy it; I did! Well – most of it!

Ted Hold
March 2004

Chapter 1 The Seed is Sown

My dad had been a soldier in the First World War, No. 75879. Pte. Edward Hold, 4th. Battalion Northumberland Fusiliers. He was badly wounded and taken prisoner. German doctors saved his life. He may have been in Sprottau prison camp as photographs exist, but not of him. I know he was set to work on a farm, minus his boots to deter escape, and was made to stamp cabbages into barrels - sauerkraut! When the war ended the farmer didn't want to let him go and refused to return his boots. My 'old man' walked back to the British lines barefoot! I learned all this as a child and remember seeing the shrapnel scars, like indented oyster shells, on his back and arms and being duly awe struck.

\#1 The Northumberland Fusiliers Brigade Engineering School Staff in 1919

Edward Hold senior, seated on the far left of the front row, became a Sergeant/Instructor after his escape from captivity at the end of WW1

A few photographs of him in uniform still exist but the P.O.W. grey 'soap', more like pumice stone, and hard bun which had to be soaked before it was edible, have long since vanished. I can remember playing with them as a child. His pay-book and medals, I am glad to say, still survive. Before demobilisation he was a Sergeant Instructor in the Northumberland Fusiliers Engineering School. After the war he worked as a chauffeur and later as one of the first drivers on Sunderland Corporation 'muck-carts' - vans with a half oval body and sliding lids. He then worked as a driver for the GPO Engineering department in Newcastle.

 # 2   Edward Hold senior and junior circa 1930

My patriotism was first aroused by my Dad taking me to the War Memorial on Armistice Day. I well remember everything coming to a stop at eleven a.m. on 11th November when the maroons were fired. I also remember, vividly, one day holding his hand and trotting by his side, being a bit late, and the maroons 'going off' when we were half way down Blandford St. We were en route of course to the War Memorial from home, 26 High Street West, opposite the Londonderry. I must have been about five or six at that time. From the moment the maroons were fired no one moved and there was complete silence - the world stood still - or so it felt until two minutes later the silence was broken by the maroons once more. Poppy wreaths, Bands, Banners, parades and medals; I loved it all.

Dad was an old Church Lads Brigade member and it was inevitable that I should join. It was still being run by Sunderland Parish Church, Holy Trinity, at the bottom of Coronation Street, where Mam and Dad were married, Dad was a sidesman, and I was baptised. I can remember going to Church with him when I was tiny and being left in the old box-pew while he went to Communion. I was alone, boxed in and only able to see the ceiling. It seemed he was gone forever and I felt deserted. I remember the strong smell of wine when, happily, he returned - my first recollection of alcohol.

My C.L.B. days sowed the first seeds of militarism. In Khaki for the first time, proudly wearing a forage cap with a badge very like the Victoria Cross. Rifle drill, foot drill, competitions, games and team spirit followed. One of the games we played was 'Paddy Sez', which contributed a great deal to mental alertness. Parades and drills were held in the old Mission Hall in Flag Lane off Coronation Street where the Sunday School was also held. We also drilled on occasion in the Assembly Garth where, so I was led to believe, a Ball was held in honour of the Duke of Wellington. Only the Church now remains.

Every year on Empire Day we marched from the Church, up Coronation Street, and through the town to Barnes Park. All the youth organisations were on parade and we sang patriotic songs, listened to patriotic speeches, marched, countermarched and generally had a good time.

One year I got to play the Kettledrum, which, for a little titch as I was, proved very big and very heavy. I set off proudly at the head of the column banging away on my drum - and I really could play, but halfway up, and the operative word is "up", Coronation Street, I became aware that I was being overtaken by the 'columns of four'. Despite hissing, "Get back, get back, I'm supposed to be at the front", I was eventually 'swallowed up' and at the top of Coronation Street found myself at the rear of the parade.

"HALT", rang out the command, loud and clear. Then to my utter despair and humiliation the leader said, "I think you had better give that drum to one of the bigger boys." I cried all the way to Barnes Park.

We also held church parades and I well remember a visit by a Bishop. I was in the balcony in the middle of the church above the main aisle. At the end of the service, just as the Bishop was about to pass underneath me, the hymn we were singing had got to "Angels and Archangels". The "Arch" is pronounced "Ark", as in Noah's Ark, but I wanted the Bishop to hear me and, I sang in my piping treble, "Arch" as in Marble Arch. He did hear me, and lifting his head up to where I was standing continued the movement until he was gazing heavenwards as if to say, "Dear Lord, where did you find him?"

We went camping, under canvas bell tents, each year and I remember one year at Seaton Sluice we 'caught' a shark. Actually it was washed in by the tide, with a gash in its side and dead, but the sight of a dorsal fin flopping around in the waves convinced us otherwise. When the truth was tentatively established, we dragged it ashore by the tail, and tried, unsuccessfully, to cut the dorsal fin off as a trophy with our dinner knives. 'Sir', decided it should be buried, which internment was duly carried out. The next tide of course washed it out and took it further along the beach towards Blyth. It was buried again, only this time, deeper. The next tide we got a repeat performance and how we were enjoying the fun. It was finally laid to rest under the then wooden pier at Blyth and covered with rocks and for all I know it is still there - but I doubt it.

Cotherstone was another favourite camp site and it was there that I achieved a great victory. Thanks to my upbringing I was always well spoken and well mannered, dressed as neatly as circumstances permitted, clean and pretty well behaved, so among the Eastenders I became a target! I was also disinclined to fight in deference to my mother's constant pleadings, "don't get into a fight." I duly obeyed and avoided confrontation and as a result was nicknamed 'Jessie'! They were mostly tougher than me and streetwise, which I was not, and I soon learned to duck, twist, weave and dodge and I was pretty fast on my feet. It all came in handy when the physical 'games' got rough but - back to Cotherstone.

One day on an organised run around the camp area - shades of things to come - I found myself being continuously tripped from behind by one of my regular tormentors whose name, I think, was Donkin. Eventually I'd had enough and I turned and went for him. Rolling around on the ground trying to kill each other we were grabbed by the scruff of the neck by 'Sir', who I think was Mr. Stewart the Rector, and told, "You will finish this tonight in the ring."

"Tonight" happened to coincide with Parents' visiting day. Sadly, mine were not present. I wished they had been because I always felt that my Dad would have been proud of me instead of being disappointed that his firstborn was not as tough as he would have liked. I could be wrong but that was how I felt then. Anyhow, a boxing ring was made with corner seats, bucket, sponge and all. Gloves were produced and the C.L.B. settled down to see me get slaughtered.

Round One: Donkin came out intent on murder and I duly ducked, weaved, dodged and back pedalled and survived without being hit. Everyone was shouting for Donkin.

Round Two: Having learned how to survive the onslaught I tried a few tentative jabs and found I could hit him, his reactions being much slower than mine. Gaining confidence I landed a few good blows and by the end of the round I had half the camp on my side.

Round Three: Now he was going to pay for all the humiliation I'd suffered and I went for him good and proper and, big as he was, I punched him round the ring. The lads were now on their feet shouting for me and finally a right hand haymaker to his left temple, delivered with all my hate, flattened him. He was out cold!

They picked him up and carried him into his tent and laid him on his bed. I was declared the winner and given a big bottle of lemonade as a prize. I went into the tent where he was being brought back into the land of the living and being so glad to see him still alive, 'cos I really thought I'd killed him, I gave him the bottle of lemonade! Nobody called me 'Jessie' anymore!

In those days a big bottle of lemonade was something you just didn't get. A small bottle, if you were lucky, but a big bottle, no way. Which is why, when we had a leader called Mr. Renwick, I had one of those days when I wouldn't have changed places with the King - I was the King! Mr. Renwick took us on an outing to Penshaw Monument and provided the eats. For the first time in my life I had, all to myself, a BIG bottle of lemonade and a whole pork pie and am sitting on top of the world - well Penshaw Hill - monarch of all I surveyed. The memory has stayed with me to this day. Many years later I learned that he had a pork shop in Penshaw area but that in no way detracted from his generosity or that marvellous day. This of course all took place in the late twenties when times were pretty bad, especially in the North East of England. The Sunday School trips were also held at Penshaw and Coxgreen. The highlight of these occasions also being the food. A bag containing a cake, apple and/or orange, sausage roll with tea and sandwiches and sometimes sweets and a small bottle of pop.

One day we got a new Rector who disbanded the C.L.B. and turned us into Cubs - more expense for Mam; God bless her, I got a cap and jersey. Militarism was out and I learnt to tie myself in knots! That lasted for about one year I think.

Camp fires were a regular and eagerly looked forward to feature of our days under canvas. Stories were told, games played, cocoa drunk and of course camp-fire songs sung.

Being top choir boy at St Aidan's Church, Grangetown, I had a good treble voice and figured prominently in all the vocal activities. One song I used to sing solo was called 'Carry On'.

> "When you're blue just carry on
>
> Troubles are only bubbles that fade away
>
> Smile and simply carry on
>
> Where there's a smile no sorrow can ever stay
>
> Even in the darkest hours
>
> Remember the night is followed by the dawn
>
> Whenever you feel blue, here's all you've got to do
>
> Carry on, carry on, carry on."

Which, of course, I continue happily to do. Another favourite was a round.

> "I went to the animal fair, the birds and the beasts were there.
>
> By the light of the moon, the big baboon was combing his auburn hair.
>
> The monkey fell out of its bunk, and slid down the elephant's trunk.
>
> The elephant sneezed and fell on his knees
>
> and what became of the monkey – monkey – monkey - monkey" etc.

- while another group took up the refrain.

One night, I think at Seaton Sluice, sitting round the campfire the leader asked if anyone had any ideas for any new competitive game we could all join in. Ever eager to show off at something I thought I would win, I suggested - a singing competition. Well I thought it was a good idea!!!

At the same camp we were taken to the cinema in Blyth as a treat. The film was Lena Horne in 'Stormy Weather', which I enjoyed very much, particularly the singing. I think it must have been sometime in the very early thirties. Little did I know then that in 1944 I was to watch that film again in very different and most unusual circumstances; even to the extent of being involved in it's presentation - but more of that later.

Sadly it all ended in my early teens when I was a pupil at West Park Central School. Names that come to mind - Clarry and Teddy Simpson, Bobby Prince, Simmy Pounder, Tommy Wake, Norman Hedinburgh, the St Columba's C.L.B., Rev. Francis Palgrave, Major Nelson, Rev. Dawson, Mr. Stewart and Mr. Renwick. In retrospect I am grateful for my C.L.B. days which taught me discipline, foot drill, rifle drill, espirit de corps, self reliance, courage in the face of adversity, love of King, Queen and Country. To obey the law, play up, play up and play the game and live by the Ten Commandments especially, "Honour thy father and thy mother that thy days may be long in the land which the Lord thy God giveth thee." In short do as your parents tell you or get your head knocked off! My parents taught me that and none of it did me any harm - quite the opposite. If only it were so today!

Before leaving the early days a word or two about 'Uncle Frank' may be of interest. The Reverend Francis Temple Palgrave was the only son of Francis Turner Palgrave who, besides being the editor of 'The Golden Treasury', was also Professor of Poetry at Oxford. 'Uncle Frank', the Reverend F.T. Palgrave, was ordained at the age of 25 and held his first post as curate at Hetton, County Durham, where he stayed for three years. On leaving Durham he went to Canada as a missionary to the Stikine River Indians in British Columbia. Here he suffered severe frostbite and the story I heard was that to save his leg the Indians were obliged to carve off part of his foot. In any case it is a fact that on his return to England he became curate at the Sunderland Parish Church and he was still suffering from the effects of frostbite. The year was 1923 and I was two years old. My dad being a sidesman at the church obviously brought him into contact with Reverend Palgrave. A strong friendship was formed and 'Uncle Frank' became a regular visitor to our home.

Later on, when I was about 12 or 13, he took me on holiday to Montreuil-Sur-Mer in France – a walled 'city' which had been Earl Haig's HQ in World War 1 and had a big equestrian statue of him right in the middle of the town square. I remember walking around the ramparts and feeding the hens and rabbits in the 'hotel estaminet' back yard and being upset when a rabbit went missing only to turn up on the menu.

I also remember staying with him and his sister in Kensington en route to France and going to a restaurant for dinner – a first for me. Very rich tomato soup was followed by meat & veg. and a very sickly caramel pudding to finish with. It was all too much for me and I just managed to get out of the restaurant in time. Not a very good advert I'm afraid but not being used to such rich food I just couldn't help it.

Dear 'Uncle Frank', even after he retired and went to live in Dorset he kept in touch with the family. I still have letters sent by him in the late 1940s. A very kind man who was remembered with affection by all who knew him, particularly the older parishioners in Hetton and Sunderland. He died in January 1955 aged 90.

Chapter 2   Sunderland P.O. Home Guard

When I left school round about 14 – 15 years old I got a job as a butcher-boy, delivering orders, scrubbing chopping blocks, sweeping floors and spreading sawdust, cleaning windows, paring bones and making sausage for Cowling in Villette Road. My next job was with Meddes Brothers Furniture Shop in Hylton Road. General dogsbody and delivering furniture by handcart – uphill and then upstairs – try it! After that I was with Lloyds Radio Shop in Bridge Street delivering and installing radio sets. Mains electricity was the thing – no more accumulators and batteries! I then had a job car washing at Howey's Garage, Harbour View, Roker. Wet and freezing! All this was to try and augment the family income – the family was by now seven strong.

I was still washing cars on September 3rd 1939 when war was declared, the sirens sounded and Howey's staff jumped into a car inspection pit to take shelter. Of course nothing happened, the 'all clear' eventually sounded and everything came back to normal.

On September 15th my Dad died of massive pneumonia. He was 39 years old and I was 18. I was at his bedside in the Royal Infirmary as he died and my world fell apart After having tried, without success, to get a job with the GPO for many years, I was now given a job as a labourer and was the principal wage earner.

The Sunderland Post Office Home Guard was formed by the joint staffs of the Postal and Engineering sides. Not unnaturally officers and N.C.O.s were chosen from 1st World War Veterans. The Captain and the Lieutenant were Postal Inspectors. The R.S.M. being also Postal. The Sergeants were a mixture from both departments. I of course was a Private and into khaki for the second time, but not quite yet as we didn't even have an armband to begin with. We 'got fell in' in the back yard of Telephone House, St Thomas Street, and were drilled using underground cable rods as rifles.

In time we were issued with Local Defence Volunteers 'L.D.V.' armbands which soon became known as Look, Duck and Vanish. Gaiters were the next piece of equipment to arrive followed by uniforms and 13th Northumberland and Durham Home Guard flashes. Then we were kitted out with webbing and the final touch was the issue of a Canadian Ross rifle. We could now stand guard at the front door (inside) and at the back gate (locked), which we did at all times. The Linesman's Room doubled as a Guard Room and I think we got extra pay for night duty. We were still of course doing our normal GPO duties during the day. Push buttons were installed back and front and an Alarm Bell fitted in the 'Guard Room'. Let Hitler come, we were ready! In years to come I was to split my sides laughing at 'Dad's Army', it was all so true to type.

Having been lectured on tactics and field craft we decided one day to put it all into practice and off we went on manoeuvres to Warden Law, which was a copse of trees between Seaham and Houghton. We split into two teams, one defending and the other attacking. No ammunition, not even blanks, and after much crawling about and "Bang, your dead" the attackers won the day. Or had they? On return to HQ Telephone House for a post mortem, one of the chaps, Ossie Harvey, listened to all the arguments both for and against and then wound it all up by saying, "You've got it all wrong you know, the attackers didn't win! I was sitting up a tree and shot them all as they came into the wood."

There were many other Home Guard units in the town and one particular weekend they were all put to the test by the 'Powers that be'. The Army were going to test the Sunderland Home Guard defences by invading the town. We knew which weekend it was going to be but not exactly when! I was positioned in the shrubbery adjacent to the H.P.O. at the top of Coronation Street, and I was loaded with thunder flashes, awaiting the invasion. I was frozen stiff and shivered all night waiting for something to happen. Came the dawn and not long afterwards around the corner from Athenaeum Street came a soldier on a pushbike. At last my big chance to make an impact and I leaped out of the shrubbery, ignited a thunder flash and blew him off his bike, at the same time shouting, "You're dead." I got a torrent of abuse as he got back on his bike and pedalled off down Coronation Street. It was a soldier home on leave!

The invasion came a bit later on when Bren carriers started to come up High Street from the dock area. I, plus my thunder flashes, was grabbed by one of the officers and run round to the Havelock Cinema in Fawcett Street. From there, as each Bren carrier was about to pass Mackies Corner, I lit a thunder flash, rolled it towards them and blew them up. The last one was flying a white flag, I think it was white, but it made no difference because up it went. In the Sunderland Echo article some time later I believe reference was made to - "Zealous Home Guard blows up umpires"!

After that little bit of action we came back to 'Tele House' and a right old battle was raging in the back lane which had been blocked off with postal hand carts and engineering hand carts. I can't remember whether it was the 15th Scottish or the 51st Highland Div. who attacked but they came at us with the butts of their rifles and one or two nasty split heads resulted. Thank God the Home Guard who was on the roof tossing down sandbags was a rotten shot or someone could have been killed.

During the 'invasion' a plane circled the town dropping flour bombs and 'wiped out' the Power Station, Railway Station, Telephone House, etc. Years later I was to meet the navigator, Peter Nichol, who told me he had pinpointed all the targets - a Sunderland lad of course.

Now and then our alertness and abilities would be put to the test and I remember one occasion when Sergeant Billy Lloyd spotted a stranger getting out of the lift carrying a tool bag and challenged him. Something didn't seem right. The stranger tried to push his way past but was wrestled to the floor and eventually tied to a chair. Interrogation followed and he confessed eventually to being a saboteur and that we were too late as he had been all round the building planting 'bombs'. Then came the question, how had he got into the building in the first place? He had rung the bell and shown the guard his pass and he'd been let in - Simple! We had a look at his pass and very official it looked too, Home Office seal and crown and all, giving him complete access to everything and it was signed - by Adolf Hitler! Dear Dad's Army! I think we failed that particular test but it taught us a valuable lesson, which of course was the whole point of the exercise.

Besides shooting on the Rifle Range at Whitburn with our Ross rifles and .303 ammo we also practised in the .22 range underneath the H.P.O. in Sunniside. We also ran a regular weekly sweepstake from which I was eventually banned - I was winning too frequently! During my Home Guard days I was a member of the rifle team and took part in many inter-unit competitions, shooting in our own range under the H.P.O. and in the .22 range at Sunderland Police Station. One day I was dropped from the team but decided I would still go to the police station to support them. I got there by way of the Blandford Arms in Blandford Street where, to drown my sorrows and disgust at having been dropped, I downed three pints of Vaux Double Maxim. On arriving at the range I was greeted with open arms, someone had failed to turn up and I was on the team again. We lost but it wasn't my fault because I scored a 'possible', 100! Moral - if you want to score a ton, drink Double Maxim. I had wondered if Vaux would reward me for that plug but alas it's now too late as Vaux Brewery no longer exists!

One day a 'Bombing Course' was offered to the Unit and nobody wanted to go. I suppose they didn't want to miss any overtime. I, on the other hand, jumped at the chance and volunteered. So off I went accompanied (or should that have been chaperoned?) by Sergeant Bill Sumner. The course was run by the Regular Army; Royal Engineers, Uniacke Barracks, Pennypot Lane, Harrogate. We were trained in the preparation and use of the '36' grenade, anti-personnel mines and anti-tank mines. We also did field craft and I had a marvellous time.

3   The Home Guard Bombing Course in December 1940

While we were learning all there was to know about the '36' grenade we also had to learn how to throw them. Elementary you might think, but it wasn't just "pull the pin out and throw", there was a drill to follow. Holding the grenade in the palm of your hand with the fingers around the lever and against your thigh you then put the middle finger of your other hand through the ring of the safety pin. You prepare to throw by pulling the grenade away from the pin, keeping your other hand still. Your arm is now behind you ready to throw, and over it comes. All achieved in two movements thus saving time and, if in the prone position, exposure to enemy fire.

We did a lot of practising from the prone position, getting onto one knee for the actual throw, using unarmed grenades. We didn't just throw them anywhere however. We had to get enough height and enough distance to get them over a crossbar, resembling a rugby goal in structure, about 10' to 12' high and 30' or more away and onto a target at the far side. In fact we had to try and get them into the target which was - a bucket! With a '36' grenade weighing about 1.5 lb it was no mean feat but we had a lot of fun trying. Did I manage to get it into the bucket? No, but I did hit it once or twice!

It wasn't all fun though and it was here that one prize 'Willick' managed to drop a live grenade next to the Sergeant and I in the bombing bay.

The bay was like a box within a box made largely of sandbags. The outer wall had an entrance in the middle, you could then turn left or right along a corridor, go round the next wall and back on yourself. Immediately on your left or right depending on which way you were turned was a solid wall of sandbags, arm upraised height. Immediately behind that wall, although you couldn't see it, was a bank of earth sloping down to a field. 'Willick' stood on the left, I stood on the right and the Sergeant was in the middle. On the command "Prepare to throw" the right hand pulled the grenade from the pin which was left on the middle finger of the left hand, or if you were left handed vice versa. On the command "Throw" over came your arm and you released the grenade which sailed over the wall and exploded harmlessly down the slope. We'd done it in practice but this was 'live'.

The height of the wall was such that it didn't really take any effort to get the grenade over the top, which it didn't for the Sergeant and I. 'Willick' however held onto his grenade, banged his hand on the top of the sandbags, and dropped the grenade at his feet. The Sergeant and I looked at the grenade then at each other, shot out of the bay, looked at each other again, realised 'Willick' was still inside, shot back in, grabbed 'Willick' and practically carried his petrified body outside just before the grenade exploded. A real 'Willick' but still alive!

I believe he'd been a librarian's assistant in Civvy Street. During a discussion one day on the best place to put him so as not to cause any trouble to anyone else I suggested a lighthouse! From one of the lads came "and what's the Merchant Navy done to you?" During conversation with an old comrade years later I mentioned 'Willick' and was told "Oh! He finished up on the Isle of Wight."

It was also here that I met a Sergeant Instructor who was demonstrating how the anti-personnel mine that he held had so little charge in it that you could pound it with your other hand with complete safety. It blew two of his fingers off! We got the message!!!

One of the lads took very ill one day and he was in great pain. I got him to the M.O. who sent for an ambulance and I saw him safely into hospital. It was appendicitis. Coming back to camp I went to the Company Office and told the Major what I'd done and asked permission to phone the lad's mother. He sat and listened as I spoke to her and put her mind at rest and gave her all the information I could. When I put the phone down and thanked the Major he asked if I knew the lad in hospital and seemed surprised when I said no. He then surprised me by saying how impressed he was with my handling of the situation and would be sending his commendation to my C.O.

One day, during my peregrinations around the camp, I had observed posters advertising a forthcoming attraction, a performance of Mozart's 'Cosi Fan Tutti'. I, of course, wanted to see it. The only trouble was I was broke. Later on another poster appeared advertising a shooting contest, open to all, to be held a day or two before the opera. The entrance fee was 6d or 1/-, I forget which, and there were cash prizes, which I've also forgotten. It was too good an opportunity to miss so I borrowed 6d off Bill Sumner entered the Camp Shooting Competition and won! I repaid Bill, saw 'Cosi Fan Tutti' and had enough left over for a meal and a pint at the NAAFI. Life was sweet!

All the while we were there the Royal Engineers were getting on with their own every day business and training and now and then we had a chance to observe real soldiers. On one occasion, passing the Parade Ground we stopped to watch one group being drilled, or rather inspected, by a young officer. Came the command "For Inspection, Port Arms" and they duly obliged. Having passed down the line of soldiers, peering down each rifle barrel 'en passent', he then turned and opened his mouth to give the next command which should have been, "Ease Springs." Alas! He just couldn't remember what it was and stood there opening and closing his mouth for all the world looking like a goldfish! He knew what he wanted them to do however because eventually he managed to get out the command "Rattle Bolts"! Exit Home Guard with a big chuckle!

The examination at the end of the course was rigorous having to lecture the lecturers and answer all their questions with authority and satisfactorily. It had to be right; lives were at stake with live ammo being handled by virtual amateurs. I passed with flying colours. When I left Uniacke barracks I was very proficient and professional - a qualified bombing instructor with live ammo!

Back in Sunderland I was asked to present myself at the C.O.'s office in the H.P.O. The two officers had my report from Harrogate and I was asked to sit down. "Well Teddy" said one of them, "You've done extremely well and we've got an excellent report and you've qualified as a Bombing Instructor and that carries the rank of Sergeant!" or words to that effect. His next words stunned me. "I'm afraid however that we can't give you three stripes as the other Sergeants have threatened to resign if we do." How's that for Dad's Army? At work you see they were all my superiors. So even though I had qualified for Sergeant I was only made up to Corporal.

I had my day however! Lecturing the squad on the '36' grenade I had just explained how, when the lever had been released the spring forced the striker to hit the .22 cap with such force as to explode it, ignite the fuse and thereby detonate the grenade, when I was challenged by Sgt. Tot Milburn (incidentally, my boss at the time). He claimed I was talking rubbish and that he could let the striker down gently so as not to explode the cap. It was he, of course, who was talking rubbish and I said so and explained why - the shortness of the striker and the strength of the spring. I was told I was just a "young sprog" and didn't know it all and he was more experienced than I. The squad were enjoying the confrontation and sat there grinning. I tried patiently to explain once more but to no avail. At last, patience exhausted and my integrity and authority as an instructor on the line, I broke the Golden Rule of 'Safety First'.

I said, "All right Mr. Milburn", and got a '36' grenade and armed it. I then handed it to him and said, "This is a live grenade; let's see you let it down gently; but before you do - everybody else OUT OF THE ROOM", and I opened the door!   "There's no need to be like that", said Tot, putting the grenade down carefully, and I knew I'd won. Perhaps I shouldn't have done it, but I'd taken enough. It was one thing to deny me three stripes but it was quite another to put lives at risk by undermining my authority as a bombing instructor just to re-assert his own at work. "Young sprog"? Perhaps, I was just 19 but I knew my job, had proved it, and continued to do so. From then on I had no more trouble from anybody - Home Guard wise.

When the grenades arrived they were smothered in thick grease and had to be thoroughly cleaned and inspected. There must be no impediment to the smooth operation of the striker or lever. The thin wall between the cap and detonator compartment must also be checked for pinholes which would result in premature explosion immediately the lever is released. This was checked by holding the grenade, minus striker, spring and base cap, up to the light covering the base of the striker compartment with the thumb and looking into the detonator compartment for light shining through. On our first inspection I found one defect and confirmed two more - thus saving lives, but that was part of my job.

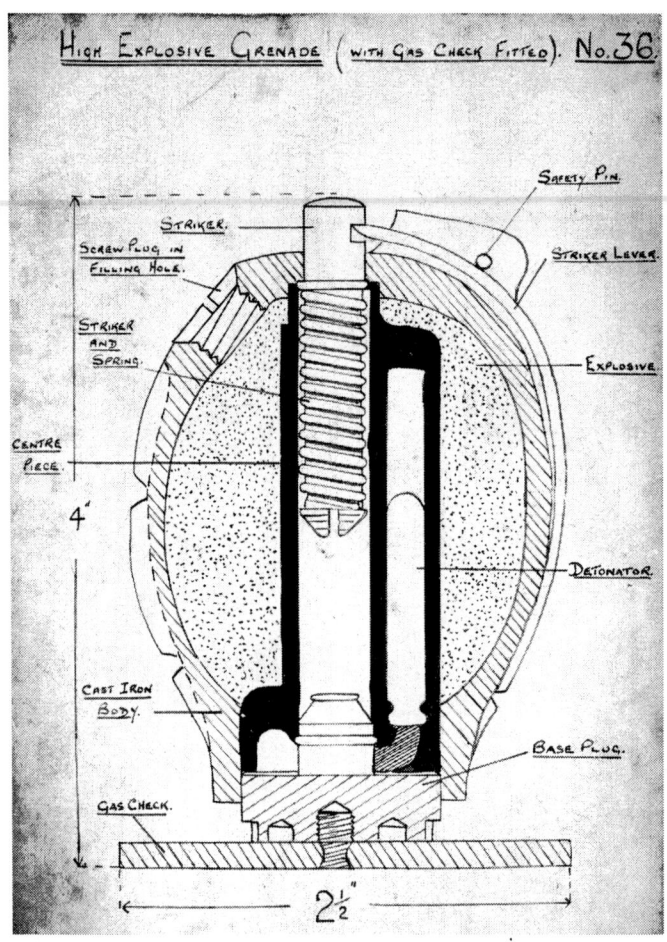

 # 4   Cross section of a '36' grenade drawn by Ted Hold in December 1940

The squad got a 'Blacker Bombard' and 'Northover Projector' – a spigot gun and anti-tank weapon. We used to practice in the fields at Whitburn on the cliff top near to the rifle range. I remember the Projector looking like a horizontal stovepipe. It fired 'ginger beer' bottles filled with phosphorus. The target was usually a stick stuck in the ground from which fluttered a white cloth. The idea was to hit the stick, which represented a tank, the bottle would break and the phosphorus set fire to the 'tank track'. I heard years later that the farmer sued the War Office for poisoning his cows. We also threw live grenades over the cliff top onto the beach which was a reserved area, sealed off to the public with barbed wire. Fulwell quarry was another bombing site.

Walking home to Grangetown after Guard duty one night an air raid was in progress. Just before reaching the synagogue in Ryhope Road I heard the bombs whistling down and was sure they were on top of me. In front was a WAAF who stood frozen to the spot. I yelled "Down!" and grabbed her, flattening her as I did so. There was a series of explosions and they were close! On standing up I saw the sky lit with flames around the Barley Mow Park Area. After making sure the WAAF was O.K. I went to see what I could do.

The bombs had fallen at the junction of Corporation and Villette Roads. Valley Road school was destroyed, the houses opposite demolished and a gas main was blazing away. A tram car stood right on the corner, not one window intact. The driver's face was a mess, full of glass splinters and all the passengers in a state of shock. The badly wounded were taken away by ambulance. Those who were able were escorted home and I took one old lady to her house in the Hastings Street area. When we arrived she discovered her bag was missing. I got a description, went back and told the police and we found it and returned it to her - her relief was good to see. By then the A.R.P. and police had everything under control and, being surplus to requirements, I went home.

I was a member of the Home Guard for about three years but really wanted to join the army. I was itching to get into the war and 'do my bit'. The GPO was, to some extent, a reserved occupation so I started to send 'memos' to Staff Group asking to be released for military service. I kept getting negative replies but eventually got one which said "Please don't send any more memos as you will be getting called up soon" - I waited, impatiently. Eventually my calling-up papers arrived, I passed the medical A1, got my railway warrant and off I went!

I enjoyed 'Dad's Army', but I should have been a SERGEANT!

Chapter 3   Royal Corps of Signals

It was a miserable wet evening as I stepped onto the platform of Ossett Railway Station on November the 5th 1942 to become a soldier in H.M. forces. There were about 30 of us, mostly ex GPO engineers and a few of us were acquainted. We got 'fell in' and marched up the ramp/steps to Station Road and then on to the 4th Battalion KOYLI Drill Hall, about a mile or so away, where we were quickly allocated bunk beds and kitted out and introduced to denims, webbing, brasses, blanco, mepo, army boots and polish! I already knew my army number 14328664.

The next six weeks were spent being shouted at, bullied, coerced and licked into shape. Rifle drill, foot drill, bayonet and target practice, field craft, assault course, aptitude tests and marching. We marched into Ossett and back for breakfast, dinner and tea, I reckon at least six miles a day, and we had to sing! And it was "Swing those arms shoulder height." The only bit I didn't enjoy was having to clean, blanco and polish our webbing, belt, ammo pouches, rifle sling, gaiters and packs small and large and of course our boots every night. It wouldn't have been so bad if we hadn't been crawling on our bellies in muddy November soaked fields every day and having a bunch of sadists for NCOs!

I didn't enjoy the inoculation parade either, nor did anyone else. We were marched into Ossett to one of the mills, a big empty hall, stripped to the waist and stood in 2 or 3 queues which slowly moved forward to the M.O.'s table. En route an orderly rubbed everyone's left shoulder with 'spirit' another orderly rubbed on some 'bugs' and the third one scratched the same spot, breaking the skin - that was our vaccination. We continued to move forward to receive two 'jabs' - that was our inoculation. After all that we got dressed and returned to the Drill Hall. It was like being on an assembly line!

The moans and groans and cries of agony during the night would have done credit to Dante's Inferno as we turned in our sleep onto the swollen and extremely painful tortured arms. Worse was to come. Next morning movement was excruciating and getting dressed next to impossible. Then came the march to breakfast - "Swing those arms", "Get the blood circulating", "Left, Right, Left, Right", "Swing and sing", "The more you swing those arms the better it will be." And so it proved - eventually! The proving, however, was very, very painful

On the subject of singing once again, I was in my element with 'In the Q.M.'s Stores', 'I've got sixpence', 'Tipperary', 'Pack Up Your Troubles' and 'Ten Green Bottles'. I even introduced a variation which became very popular. After, "and if ten (etc.) green bottles should accidentally fall", came, "Tinkle, Tinkle, Tinkle, CRASH!! There'd be nine (etc.) green bottles hanging on the wall." It fitted the step and the mood..

Each intake was split into Sections which competed against each other and earned themselves points for performance. They also earned 'fatigues' for losing points and we had a right 'Willick' in our Section. He couldn't assemble his webbing properly, couldn't march in step and taking a bolt out of a rifle and replacing it remained a mystery to him for the whole six weeks.

 # 5   Raw recruits at the Primary Training Centre Ossett in December 1942
Ted is seated third from the right in the second row

To avoid being on permanent fatigues, we 'carried' him, dressed him, undressed him and made sure he wasn't going to drop us in it. He came in for a lot of criticism and dire threats from the Section. I remember he came to me one day and said, "They", (meaning our Section), "are threatening to paint a swastika on my behind; you will help me to resist wont you?" to which I replied "No I won't, in fact I'll bloody well help them" - He was most upset!

One of the lads was a lay preacher, young as he was, and each night he got down on his knees by the side of his bunk and said his prayers. He came in for a lot of ribald comments and heckling from one or two of the less enlightened of the species but he stuck to his principles and never once wavered and eventually earned everyone's respect and I admired him for it. I believe he got permission to preach at a local chapel on Sundays - he certainly went to Church. I've got the feeling all of us but him were confined to barracks until very late on in our training.

Apart from sticking bayonets into swinging straw stuffed bags we had another delightful exercise designed to make us efficient executioners or defenders. We all stood in the field in a circle with rifle and sheathed bayonet, on guard. The Sergeant stood in the centre holding in both hands a long bamboo pole on one end of which was a turnip sized pompom and on the other end a cloth wrapped wire ring of about six inches diameter. The exercise was that he would slowly circle on the spot and suddenly present the ring to any individual who then had to lunge at it and thrust his bayonet through the middle, immediately withdrawing same and standing on guard for the next move. That was the presentation of the pompom which you then had to hit with the butt of your rifle i.e. bayonet the enemy, then knock his head off. Thus it was, in, out, clout and on guard. The ring and the pompom could be presented at any height in any position in any order and at any time and it certainly kept us on our toes.

One glorious, never to be forgotten day, the boot was on the other foot, so to speak. The Sergeant presented the pompom to, lets call him 'Pillick', who promptly swung his rifle up and butted the pompom good and hard. As he did so, the sheath flew off his bayonet and, as the sheath was flying over the wall and into the road, the Sergeant presented the ring by his own right boot which 'Pillick' promptly bayoneted - thus ruining a pair of boots which the Sergeant had lovingly 'honed' to a beautiful shine over many a long day. The roar could be heard in Ossett as the Sergeant chased 'Pillick' out of sight, doubting his legitimacy with every step of his bayoneted boot. We of course had a 'field day'.

While on the subject of 'Pillick' we had another – 'Pillick Mk.2' whose permanent problem was the assault course, or at least one part of it. After the barbed wire, zigzag planks and various other obstacles we faced a seven foot (or was it eight foot?) wooden wall. The only way over that was to take a running jump, hang on with your fingertips and haul and scramble with boots and knees up and over. Once on the other side, by now pretty well exhausted, you faced the final challenge, a pit about seven foot across filled with muddy water and with a sloping, slippery approach and exit. The only way over that was to run like hell and launch yourself across getting ready to grab dry land and stop yourself sliding back into the mud. 'Pillick Mk.2' used to run like hell, inexplicably stop on the edge and then jump, right into the mud. He always did the same thing every time and never learned to run and launch himself, letting his own impetus carry him across. He always ran to the edge, stopped and jumped into the mud.

On our 'Final' assault the instructor was determined to get him across and grabbed Pillick Mk.2's hand after he came over the wall and yelled, "Right! Run with me! Run! Run! Run!", then, "Now JUMP!" and off into the air sailed the instructor. 'Pillick Mk.2' stopped dead on the edge, still holding the hand of the instructor who was jerked to a stop in midair. Gravity did the rest and 'Pillick Mk.2', still hanging on tightly, was pulled down the slippery slope into the mud alongside the instructor who had been, up until that moment, wearing immaculate white singlet and flannels. The instructor on this hilarious occasion was an officer and, if memory serves me right, his name was Tilly. I'm not sure how he felt!

We were kept so busy that we had little leisure time. In any case after the day was over we had all the mud to remove from denims, webbing and boots and then it was blanco, spit and polish, and clean rifles. Bed was heaven! Reveille? I can't remember whether it was 6 or 7 a.m. but it was then wash, shave, dress, make your bed, blankets and spare kit, look regimental and on parade for inspection. That was followed by whatever torture and then the march into Ossett for breakfast. On returning the training took its natural course until, into and out of Ossett for dinner, more training, then in and out for tea, Singing and Swinging all the way. Then it was cleaning up time again.

As I say we were kept very busy. I do remember, however, at least one occasion going into Ossett to the cinema. It coincided with being issued with our first battledress; up to now of course it had been denims. I think it must have been pretty near the end of our six weeks training and crawling around in the mud. Anyhow the battledresses were as stiff as cardboard and had whitish streaks all over them, apparently they had been impregnated with some sort of anti-gas chemical. After sitting in the cinema for an hour or so our eyes began to smart and we found ourselves with tears running down our cheeks. The heat of our bodies had warmed up the anti-gas chemical and released some sort of vapour which wasn't doing our eyes any good at all. Needless to say we got out in hurry. I could just imagine the locals saying, "That must have been a good picture, it's even set the soldiers crying." Sadly I don't remember what the picture was.

At the end of it all we had various tests for aptitude and intelligence; practical, oral and written. Our six weeks 'work' had been monitored and assessed and, together with the final 'exams' we were put into various categories and I was recommended for O.C.T.U. - Officer Cadet Training Unit. I was delighted. My C.L.B. and Home Guard training and my own keenness and ability had paid off. Pride however, as is well known, comes before a fall. One of the last things I did, prior to going before a Colonel's Board to be finally passed for O.C.T.U., was to fill in a form. Among the questions were: "University, College or Public School Attended?", "Educational Qualifications?", "Name And Address Of Bank?".

I was posted to the 3rd Trades Training Battalion (3 T.T.B.), Royal Corps of Signals, Huddersfield, and was billeted in a Mission Hall somewhere off the main New Street. It had double tier wooden bunk beds, two toilets and one urinal in a tiny outside yard for about 100 men. Washing facilities were equally primitive - and it was a wet and miserable winter. Bathing facilities were available at the Public Baths, parading for that purpose. I was fortunate with my billet as most of the others were in old mills which had been condemned in the First World War, so I heard - and could believe!

There was one I remember, called Fittons Building, equally dilapidated. We ate in yet another old mill and the food was prepared in less than sanitary conditions. Most of the buildings were rat-infested and when on fatigues, peeling mountains of potatoes, turnips, carrots, cabbages or whatever, we used to amuse ourselves by flicking our knives up into the hessian ceilings and watch the impressions made by the rats as they scurried round the top side of the hessian. Muck was everywhere and trying to keep yourself clean for morning parade while doing an all night spud bashing duty was extremely difficult - as I found out one morning when I was put on my first '252' (charge) for having dirty gaiters. Fortunately I was subsequently just admonished.

I think the place we paraded in was called Silver Street. I have a memory of Sergeant Major Hargrieves bringing us to 'Attention' in Silver Street, marching the length of the pavement; halting and 'about turning'. Nothing very unusual in that, except that, whilst his legs were still in the corkscrew position and before he brought his left boot crashing down alongside his right, he reached behind with his right hand and vigorously scratched his backside grimacing as he did so. Not on the right cheek, not on the left cheek but right in the groove - for quite a long time - before finally crashing to attention! He went through the same pantomime every day. We reckoned he had itchy piles or a tapeworm. Nobody of course ever enquired!

Oh! I almost forgot The Colonel's Board and O.C.T.U. The first week I was at Huddersfield I was marched into the C.O.'s office and there was the Colonel, Adjutant, and another. My impression was that they were already totally disinterested. One was looking at papers on the desk, one was twiddling with something or other, I've forgotten what, and the other one asked questions, the answers to which they already had on my form. I remember another question I'd answered which they asked again, would I accept a commission in any branch of the Army other than the Royal Corps of Signals?

My reply again was, "I'd rather be commissioned in the Regiment for which I've been trained." I failed the Colonel's Board and I don't think I was ever in with a chance. Ability and potential counted for little without a good education and a good bank balance. I was very disappointed, I would have loved to have been an officer. With hindsight of course they were right - how could I have paid for uniforms and mess bills etc. on basic pay, even officer's pay. At the time, and for years after, I felt cheated and was quite bitter but consoled myself with the thought that perhaps it was all for the best. As an officer I would have been somewhere else in the war and might have been killed. I think being rejected dampened my enthusiasm more than the lousy weather we suffered.

The Signals Training School was housed in the Town Library and we went there for lectures and Morse Code training, if you could keep awake. There were so many buildings that needed guards and fire-pickets, so many fatigues that needed to be done that no one got away with more than the odd night or two off duty. Even then it paid you to get out of Huddersfield if you had any spare time, or you would be grabbed for duty by 'press gangs' who roamed the streets looking for victims.

There was also a workshop near the tram sheds not far from Huddersfield Football Ground where we learned to repair radio sets, solder, wire and generally tinker. Learning to be an Electrician Signals, Radio Mechanic or Instrument Mechanic, all of which I subsequently achieved, would have been a much easier and more pleasant business had it not been for the never-ending round of guards and fatigues which sapped the energy and enthusiasm. The most degrading and filthiest job I ever had to do was - on a Sunday of all days - bag a stinking, festering, maggot- infested mountain of bones - with bare hands! I only did it once as I found an escape route. The Battalion formed a choir under one Corporal Leslie Suggett, and they advertised for members. Practices were held on Sunday mornings as well as other times and members were excused fatigues to attend practices. Whoopee! No more stinking bones for me and I volunteered.

"What sort of voice have you?", said Corporal Suggett.

"I've no idea", said I, "I haven't sung since I was a boy soprano."

Marching to and from Ossett was forgotten. Corporal Suggett struck a chord on the piano and invited me to sing up the scale, he then stuck another chord a tone higher and I duly obliged again. After the third chord yet one more tone higher he said, "You're a Tenor", and thus was born Ted Hold, 'Tenor'.

Life became more tolerable from then on and, in due course, the choir sang 'Jesu, Joy of Man's Desiring' in the Parish Church and we gave a concert at which I sang 'There'll Always Be An England' backed by the choir. The highlight however was when the choir were going to perform at a service in Queen Street Mission and the week before the performance the soloist was whipped into hospital. Leslie Suggett grabbed me and took me to a music shop in the High Street and looking in the window at sheet music on display said "Is there anything there you could sing?" I spotted a sacred transcription of Handel's Largo, a song called 'Light' and he bought it, we practised it and then came the great night.

The choir stalls in Queen Street Mission rise from the floor of the main Hall, in tiered rows, to the back of the church, ending with the organ top-centre - just like a section of seats in a Greek/Roman amphitheatre. The song 'Light' had a violin obbligato (as well as organ) accompaniment and one of the Battalion was providing that, standing next to Corporal Suggett the organist. I was just above floor level, on the platform which was the base for the choir stalls. It was there, sometime in early May 1943 I believe, that I sang my first real Tenor solo 'Light'.

I couldn't help noticing as I was singing the second verse that two dear old ladies sitting in the front row were crying. It was a strange feeling to know I could have that effect on people. I can't help saying now, after looking back all those years, that I hope it was genuine emotion and not that they were two music critics!

To return, for a moment, to the unpleasant side of 3 T.T.B., one day we suddenly had an epidemic on our hands almost everyone was dropping like flies and the hospital and surrounding district hospitals were full - I think it was Scarlet Fever! In the conditions under which we were living who should be surprised? And what was the army's answer? A bucket of Condy's fluid outside the cookhouse in which to disinfect your plates, knives, forks and spoons and, where the victims had slept, to sprinkle disinfectant round the bed! All this meant of course that there were very few left to do guards, pickets and fatigues and for those that were left - life was rough!!!

It wasn't all rain, pain and misery however! My wife-to-be, Ena, had joined the Army almost a year before, to get away from me she says. She was at this time stationed at the 5th Operator Training Battalion in Slaithwaite, about three miles from Huddersfield, so wasn't it kind of the Army to send me to Huddersfield? Well, I thought so! Ena had been 'adopted' by the Garside family in Slaithwaite and it was home from home for her, as it was for me once I had met them. I spent every spare moment I could with Ena and the Garsides, even singing for them in the Chapel at Crimble. It was by one of the Chapel members that I was invited to join the very famous Colne Valley Male Voice Choir who were due very soon to broadcast for the B.B.C. As my first home leave from the army, 8 days 'mid training', was due on the same week 5th February 1943 I had, however reluctantly, to decline.

 # 6   Ena and Ted in Slaithwaite in 1943

Standing one day in the bus queue in New Street waiting to go to Slaithwaite I spotted the 'press gang' coming down the street looking for victims - and quick as a flash I dived into the nearest shop and crouched behind the racks of merchandise until they had gone past. Standing up again I saw the slightly puzzled but amused looks of a couple of ladies and shop assistants and discovered I was surrounded by knickers, bras, silk stockings and various kinds of lingerie. I fled, but not into the arms of the 'press gang'.

After the first three months I failed my exams and had to do it all again. I've often wondered if it was psychosomatic. It gave me another three months to be close to Ena! In any case I proposed, bought the ring and put it on her finger in Green Head Park.

Something else, also of great significance, happened. A recruiting party from the 6th Airborne Division Signals arrived, resplendent in red berets, looking for suitably qualified volunteers - I volunteered!

I've been asked more than once why I volunteered and I don't think there is any short answer. I think the answer lies buried somewhere among the following, all valid and honest, reasons.

1. The glamour of the red beret and belonging to an elite force.

2. Extra pay. A shilling a day. My first weeks pay was 6 shillings, subsequently rising

   to 7/6, so it was almost double normal pay.

3. Giving myself a boost in Ena's estimation (I hoped).

4. To make my old man proud of me (I know, he died in 1939 - but).

5. On passing my exams I would be sent to a holding Battalion in Kirkburton and posted from there to wherever the Army thought fit - and God knows where I would end up and with whom.

Also, down at the Tram Sheds workshop one day, it had been announced that 'they' wanted an Instrument Mechanic - a superior sort of being, good with his hands who, given the raw materials, could actually make things as well as repair them. Accordingly everyone was given a piece of copper approximately $1\frac{1}{2}$" x $\frac{3}{4}$" x $\frac{1}{2}$", taps and dies, a drill with bits, calipers, file, emery paper and a segment from a commutator which had to be copied precisely. We had two days to produce the finished product. Mine was judged the best and 'they' had found their 'Instr. Mech.' The next day 'they' said an 'Instr. Mech.' was no longer required!!!

Qualified as a Sergeant in the Home Guard but..., recommended for O.C.T.U. but..., qualified as an 'Instr. Mech.' but! Was it me? In any event I think it only served to spur me on, to prove myself and maybe that is another reason why I volunteered for the 6th A/B Div. As it was to turn out I had made the right decision because the wonderful things which follow would not otherwise have happened.

So, for all those reasons, I chose to go where I decided - I volunteered for the 6th A/B Div. Sigs., passed my exams, asked Ena to wait for me, kissed her goodbye and set off for Bulford Barracks on Salisbury Plain.

Chapter 4   The Red Beret

In those nostalgic days of hissing steam, pungent smoke, burning metal and the abiding memory of clickety-clack, clickety-clack, which often lulled me to sleep, I was to travel hundreds of miles on those marvellous L.N.E.R., L.M.S. and G.W.R. regional lines courtesy of H.M. Forces. Sunderland, Newcastle, Huddersfield, Leeds, Ossett, Kings Cross, Waterloo, Bulford, Salisbury I got to know very well. Not unnaturally, the trains were crowded with Forces personnel and as the years went by they became overcrowded. Corridors were crammed and even toilets utilised as seats. Crossing the country took hours with delays, mysterious shuntings, stops and changes frequent.

Leeds in particular was a station to avoid if at all possible - delays for hours were normal. The canteen however always had tea on the go with the bottom half of cut-down bottles as mugs. On one occasion I remember falling asleep, head in arms on the canteen table. When I eventually awoke and sat up my left arm fell off the table and hit the chair one hell of a crack but I didn't feel a thing. My arm was dead, no life in it at all, I couldn't move it and I almost panicked. I'd obviously stopped the flow of blood with my head. Eventually, after what seemed a lifetime, the blood flowed again and the pins and needles became sheer pain, simply excruciating. Leeds was a place to avoid.

However here I am on my first ever Waterloo - Bulford - Salisbury trip, an exciting journey into the unknown, off to join the 6th A/B Div. Sigs. and I was keen to see what lay ahead. Many of the stations we went through reminded me very much of Will Hay and 'Oh! Mr. Porter' and one intriguing place called 'Idmiston Halt' took my fancy, it was simply a platform in the middle of nowhere.

There was a group of maybe half a dozen of us turned up at the Company Office of the 6th A/B Div. Sigs. at Bulford Camp that day, there was no reception committee and nobody seemed to care who or what we were. As we stood reading the notice board, for want of something better to do, an A/B soldier hobbled past on crutches, leg in plaster. A few minutes later yet another one came past, arm raised and elbow bent in a grotesque parody of a "Heil Hitler" salute and encased in a plaster and metal splint. At that moment a fairly small but solid Sergeant appeared on the scene, looked us over and said, "Are you the new intake?"

"Yes Sarge", we chorused, still trying to come to terms with the implications of what we'd just seen.

With a look of amused pity he tossed his head heavenwards and said, "Huh! You'd better report to Company Office", and walked away shaking his head. Meekly we obeyed and went in like lambs to the slaughter

During the first few days we were duly 'processed', completely kitted out, billeted (rectangular hut) and issued with a short Lee Enfield rifle, but most especially, issued with the famous 'red' (maroon really) beret and Pegasus shoulder flashes (printed, not silk and wool). Although I'd done nothing yet to deserve them, I had a feeling it wouldn't be long before I did and I felt very proud as I sewed them on my Battle Dress. I must have been among the last batch to volunteer, for now, up to strength, we were to fall in for our first 'Pukka' parade.

 # 7   Ted wearing the Red Beret and Airborne Flash in September 1943

Duly blancoed, polished and immaculately turned out we paraded for the first time on the A/B Signals parade ground and, as we stood at last awaiting the next command, onto the parade ground marched the R.S.M. in shirt sleeve order carrying a short baton. As we came to attention he clashed his baton on the ground and bawled in a voice which, I'm sure, must have been heard in Bulford village about a mile away, "My name is Carr and I'm a bastard." For the next three years we had no reason to doubt him.

R.S.M. Carr's face could have belonged to a boxer and his permanent scowl threatened annihilation at any moment. He didn't so much put the fear of God into us as the fear of Carr. The drill Sergeant, over whom he held sway, did his level best to please him by being every bit as tough with us as he was. At the end of the day, or rather by the beginning of D-Day, they'd done their job well and we were an extremely fit and efficient bunch of blokes who did exactly as and when told.

Not only were we good at our jobs: wireless operators, linesmen, electricians, Signals, Instrument and Radio mechanics etc., but we were also highly trained in weaponry: rifle, sten, bren, tommy gun, anti-tank gun, grenades and unarmed combat. I find it difficult now to realise I could take a rifle and bayonet away from an attacker using only my bare hands, but I could and did. The steel helmet was not only to protect your head but could also be used to bust someone's face in. The steel toe plate on your boots was also useful for kicking someone's kneecap off - all good stuff.

Part of the fitness training started in the small hours of the morning, at 6 a.m. I think. Reveille consisted of the Corporal bellowing everyone from their slumbers and trying to break the stove with a poker. On went the boots, on went the overcoat over the pyjamas and out we went to gallop round the camp perimeter in all weathers, well over a mile I would think. Back to barracks for wash (cold water) shave and get ready for breakfast. Now there was a meal, porridge, bacon, egg, tomatoes and/or baked beans, fried bread or toast, bread, butter, jam, tea. It wasn't until I did my first cook-house fatigues that I found out why the fried eggs always looked good but were more or less solid and the toast was always rubbery. The eggs had been waiting ages on the hot plate prior to serving and the 'toast' was a piece of bread rubbed across a 'red-hot' hotplate, turned over and rubbed again. Singed, not toasted! But it all went down. We used up a lot of energy and were always hungry.

Foot drill, rifle drill, always marching and running. We even ran up Beacon Hill backwards! On the top there was a little plateau and copse and once there it was, last man up the trees on fatigues, last man down the trees on fatigues and last man to reach the end of the plateau on fatigues. It was hard work until we got used to it and could I climb, jump and run? You bet I could.

I used to enjoy the rhythm and precision of slow marching, especially when serenaded by the R.S.M. whose dulcet tones once again rattled the windows in Bulford village.

"**Some** body **shit** on my **door-step**

Some body **said** it was **you**!"

"Keep those heads up, keep those arms still, backs straight!"

"**One,** two, three, **One**, two, three" etc. etc.

Before leaving R.S.M. Carr or 'TARA' as he was called (behind his back). As we filed into church one day he was heard to bellow at someone "Get your effing beret off." Once inside he excelled himself. During the sermon two of the lads started talking and unknown of course to them the R.S.M. was right behind. Tapping them on the shoulder he said, in what he imagined was a whisper but was heard by everyone in the church "Keep quiet, where's your reverence C---s!" I swear blind the padre visibly shuddered. The odd thing is I've heard similar stories from various sources over the years and have come to the conclusion that ALL R.S.M.s spring from the same peripatetic sire! R.S.M. Carr was no Sunday School teacher but he was an excellent drill instructor and disciplinarian or as he had so sweetly informed us - a bastard! But more of him later.

Meals were interspersed by drill and physical training, works parade, and unless on fatigues or guard duty the rest of the time was yours. There was a NAAFI, Cinema, Garrison Theatre, Church and Dance Hall. Amesbury and Stonehenge weren't far away and a little further on was Salisbury which I visited frequently. The summer of 1943 was glorious and being in the heart of Wiltshire on Salisbury Plain much more to be desired than the dark satanic mills of Huddersfield. As a result guards duty and fatigues were not so tedious even when it rained and they were also more evenly distributed. There were also ABCA Lectures only one of which I remember. On that particular occasion a film unit didn't turn up and C.S.M. Robson took charge.

"As we can't have our usual ABCA lecture because...", etc., "...we will now have a question and answer session and I want to see the Sergeants in a line out front." They duly complied.

"Now these men are Sergeants because of their superior intellect" - which statement was received in utter disbelief – "and they will answer any question you care to put to them", and he continued as he surveyed his captive audience, "If they can't answer your questions I will."

I must here explain that C.S.M. Robson was a supercilious sort of bloke with delusions of grandeur, full of self-esteem signifying very little. In his opinion he was a very superior being indeed. I could of course be wrong, but that was the impression he gave, not only to myself, but to at least one other. I wish I could recall his name but let's call him 'The Don'. He had been University educated and considered all N.C.O.s his mental inferiors - and why not? - and resented very deeply having to submit to their slightest ignorant whim. He was sitting in the front row totally bored with the proceedings until he heard C.S.M. Robson say "and if they can't answer your questions I will." For him it was a heaven sent opportunity and he savoured the moment.

He bided his time until a lot of questions and answers had been dealt with and just as they were beginning to dry up he rose to his feet and said, "I have a question to ask the Sergeant Major."

"Yes, yes, yes", said C.S.M. Robson ready, willing and eager to show off his intellect!

"What", said our university friend, "What is the difference between a psychiatrist and a psychologist?" and sat down. For the next two minutes or so he sat with a bland expression on his face and gazed intently at C.S.M. Robson who proceeded to talk a lot of twaddle and slowly but surely tie himself into verbal knots and, metaphorically speaking, disappear up his own orifice. It was a marvellous performance and brought that ABCA lecture to an enjoyable conclusion especially for our learned friend in the front row.

He figured in two other incidents! One day, on parade, the R.S.M. called out three names and barked, "Front and Centre." 'The Don' was one of them. R.S.M. Carr then proceeded to give them a verbal lashing for showing no real interest in anything, particularly the A/B Div. I think they must have put in for a transfer.

The R.S.M. questioned them individually. To the first one he barked, "And what the hell do you want to join?"

"The 'X' Regiment", came the reply.

"A right bloody mob", said the R.S.M.

"And you, what do you want to join?"

"The 'Y' Regiment Sir", came the reply.

"A right pansy mob", said the R.S.M.

"And you?", he said to 'The Don'.

"The A.F.S., Sergeant Major", said 'The Don'. The R.S.M. almost had an apoplectic fit.

"The A.F.S.", he screamed, "The A.F.S.? The AUXILIARY EFFING FIRE SERVICE? That's EFFING CIVVY STREET! – I want to join THAT!"

As it turned out 'The Don' stayed with the Div. A few months before D-Day the conversation got around to the possibility of being killed or wounded in action and I remember 'The Don' saying he would rather die than lose a limb. He had no wish to come back to Civvy Street minus a limb. During the Invasion he was badly wounded and had both legs amputated. According to all accounts he should have made a good recovery. Sadly he didn't! I've always felt that when he found out the extent of his injuries he just gave up and died.

To return to a more pleasant topic however, I found Salisbury a very beautiful city and I have happy memories of its wonderful Cathedral and lovely riverside walks. It was on one of these walks that a blue and orange vision flashed down river and I'd seen my first Kingfisher. It was also on the riverside that TOC H had a club and sitting by the riverbank with tea and scones on a sunny day was most peaceful.

It was at the Church Canteen in Salisbury that I spotted a poster advertising for singers, especially Tenors, to help in the local operatic society. Needless to say I joined and also became involved in Saturday night concerts in the Guildhall. One cameo sketch I recall I was dressed as a Sultan with a young harem girl on my knee singing, "Come to me my Sweet Princess, to my heart I would thee press", to the melody of 'In a Persian Market'.

Gilbert and Sullivan's 'opera', 'The Mikado', was presented by Miss Elsie Graham and her party at the Bishop Wordsworth School Hall week commencing Monday January 3rd to Saturday 8th 1944, Matinee 2.15 p.m. I was in the Chorus, it was my first operatic performance, and I enjoyed it immensely. Up till then I had always considered 'G & S' beneath me musically speaking, having been born into and brought up in the world of Grand Opera and Classical Music, but it whetted my appetite which, in years to come, I was to pretty well satisfy.

Salisbury of course was full of troops including Yanks and military police. The British M.P.s in red-topped peaked hats patrolled singly, the Yanks in white helmets (Snowdrops), patrolled in pairs - and they were all needed. The Yanks (over-paid, over-sexed and over here) had it all! More money, better uniforms and brash with it. It isn't surprising there was the odd 'scuffle'.

The Ox & Bucks Light Infantry, The Devons and the Royal Ulster Regiment formed the 6th Air Landing Brigade of glider borne light infantry - a hard lot. One St. Patrick's night the R.U.R. were in Salisbury making the most of it. On that occasion I think the British M.P.s doubled up, so did the Yanks. Waiting on the platform for the last train back to Bulford, around 11 p.m. to midnight, I observed a gang of R.U.R.s making their way up the stairs to cross the railway via the footbridge. Coming up the stairs, in the opposite direction, was a solitary Yank. He was either a very brave man or extremely trusting, in either case he continued up the stairs and across the footbridge and disappeared into the mob of R.U.R.s coming in the opposite direction. He reappeared, being held aloft by many arms, and was unceremoniously dumped over the side onto the track. Within ten minutes of the train arriving came the announcement "Owing to hooliganism the train will not be departing for Bulford." They'd wrecked it, seats ripped up, windows broken and fights galore! Unacceptable behaviour? Reprehensible? Perhaps! But they were trained up to the hilt, spoiling for a fight and raring to go. In three short months, in June, they did go and a lot of them sadly were killed.

Chapter 5   Airborne Initiative

Sergeant Bowkett, our Section Sergeant, was over 6' tall - or would have been had his head and shoulders not been permanently hunched. As a result his arms dangled slightly in front of his body. Rumour had it that he served some time in India and his shoulder muscles had been damaged by a tribesman's musket, or whatever. I could well believe it as his everyday speech, directions and orders were liberally sprinkled with Urdu, Hindu or what have you.

"Tyro bloke!" (Stop), "Hidderow Jildi" (Come here quickly), "Teek-Eye" (OK), "Kit Na Budgie?" (What's the time?). The phonetics are mine and bear no resemblance to the originals I'm sure!

He was a genial chap and well liked. He was no drill Sergeant or disciplinarian but he was one hell of an organiser. He could get a job done and was not averse to getting his hands dirty or putting his own strong shoulder to the task in hand. Anything technical however was not his metier. He might have had Signals training but if so it didn't show.

Before he arrived on the scene the 'dragon shed' where we kept all the gear like trailers, motor bikes, charging engines, camouflage nets, etc, etc, was chock-a-block. To get at anything involved a lot of climbing over things and shifting around. Bowkett changed all that and when he'd finished, or rather we'd finished, you could actually walk into the 'dragon shed' unimpeded. With the aid of hooks and ropes he'd simply hung everything up on the walls and from the ceiling. From that moment on whenever we asked him "What shall we do with this?", whatever "this" may be, we always got the same reply - "Hang it up bloke" - and it became a catch phrase in the Section.

Whenever a radio or switchboard or telephone had been repaired by M Section, Sergeant Bowkett always asked the technical details even though we knew he hadn't a clue what the answer meant. One day via a Company Office clerk we found out why he wanted to know.

Sergeant Bowkett would report to Lieutenant Gladwyn, "The set has been repaired Sah."

"What was the trouble", the C.O. would ask and Bowkett would rattle off the technical details being sure the C.O. would be duly impressed with his knowledge. Lieutenant Gladwyn I'm sure, however, knew him better than that.

One day Bowkett said to me, "What was the trouble bloke?", everybody was bloke to him.

"The dinkle switch was short-circuit Sarge", said I.

Bowkett duly reported to the C.O., "The dinkle switch was short-circuit Sah."

"Thank you Sergeant", grinned the C.O. as Bowkett saluted, about turned and disappeared. I think Rex Gladwyn enjoyed the joke as much as we did and as he knew no malice was intended no harm was done. As far as I was aware Sergeant Bowkett never found out - but later on I was to wonder!

As I said no harm was done but the same can't be said for Corporal Howard however. At the opposite end of the camp to the Company and Admin. Offices and Barracks was a collection of huts housing various workshops belonging to various Units. One of them was our

Battery Charging Shop which housed a couple of metal rectifiers, carboys of acid and distilled water, charging benches, and batteries of course. 12Volt 22 amp jobs, wireless, for the use of. Duty at this 'shop' was on a rota system and if on nights - a bunk bed was available.

The chap in charge more or less on a permanent basis was one Lance Corporal Green, inevitably christened 'Doc'! A good technician who knew his job better than anyone else and had a great sense of humour - that is until Corporal Howard appeared on the scene and was put in charge of Lance Corporal Green. Corporal Howard looked a bit like James Mason at his sneering best and managed in no time at all to alienate everyone around him, particularly 'Doc' Green. His approach and his overbearing manner was one thing but his total ignorance of anything remotely connected with charging batteries was another and in the end that ignorance helped 'Doc' Green destroy him.

One evening Doc was squatting on the floor holding a switch on one of the rectifiers and watching the needle on a meter flicker. Corporal Howard crept into the room - as was his manner - and watched over Doc's shoulder. Doc, who was aware of his presence through the glass on the meter, continued to turn the switch around and around in a clockwise direction.

After a few minutes curiosity got the better of Corporal Howard who said, "What are you doing?"

"I'm winding it up", said Doc.

"Winding it up?", said Howard.

"Of course", said Doc, "You don't think the bloody thing goes by itself do you?" Then he got up and walked away.

Some days later Doc came quietly into the same room and silently observed Corporal Howard on his knees solemnly 'Winding up' the rectifier. Doc now knew for certain the extent of Howard's ignorance and bided his time - which wasn't long in coming.

For all I know to the contrary Doc may have set the whole thing up, I wouldn't put it past him, but I was there to see and hear the 'Coup-de-Grace'. There was suddenly and inexplicably a spate of batteries failing even though they had apparently come straight from the Battery Charging Shop. It caused so much trouble that the R.M.O. sent for Corporal Howard and told him in no uncertain terms to find the cause of the problem and report back. I often wonder if it crossed Howard's mind to wonder if the rectifiers hadn't been wound up properly, but I digress.

Down to the Battery shop came Howard and told Doc that the Major wanted to know why the batteries were not holding their charge.

"You're in charge.", said Doc, "You tell him!"

"You charged the batteries so you tell me.", said Howard, "And that's an order."

"Everybody knows what's wrong, don't we", said Doc looking around. Various nods and grunts of approval came from the rest of us who were really wondering what the hell was coming next.

"Well I don't know", said Howard, "so tell me"

"Right", said Doc, "Where is this Charging Shop situated? I'll tell you, its right on the edge of the camp - and where does the mains come into the camp? - Right on the other side, miles away. And by the time the current has fed everything else in the camp what do we get down here? I'll tell you. What **we** get is a poor quality of amps! **That's** the trouble, we get a poor quality of amps. So until they move the Battery Shop to the other side of the bloody camp we'll always get a poor quality of amps and the batteries won't get properly charged!"

It was a virtuoso performance. He almost had me believing him he was so intense.

As 'Doc' Green had told Corporal Howard so Corporal Howard told the Major!!! He was promptly posted - I think - for we saw him no more. Peace reigned in the Charging Shop and there was no more trouble with the batteries.

Well, not until one night when I was on duty and, having put the batteries on charge, laid down to rest and went to sleep. Early next morning the relief arrived to find the shop and me full of sulphuric acid fumes from the batteries which were well and truly 'cooked'. Any longer and I think they would have had to bury me: instead we buried those batteries which were beyond redemption in a little plot in a field behind the shop which had been used for that purpose on more than one occasion in the past. The incident was covered up because apart from the Howards of this world we all stuck together and the 'cooked' batteries were replaced on a 'fair wear and tear' basis.

On the edge of the field in which the dead batteries lie buried was a urinal and three toilets which, apart from the obvious, were regularly used as a reading room and art gallery. Not one square inch of space on doors and walls was left bare. How many years it took to create I have no idea but as a monument to pornography it would take some beating. Most of it was sheer filth but there were also a few humerous observations e.g.

"When shitting stand upon the seat,

'cos Bulford crabs can jump six feet"

to which a second author had appended -

"If you think six feet is very high

Just go next door, the bastards fly!"

One other ubiquitous statement, apart from "Kilroy was here" and various 'Mr. Chad' remarks, was a tiny message right at the bottom of the door. You had to raise your bum from the seat and lean forward to peer very intently at this before you could read "You are now shitting at an angle of forty-five degrees." All very educational but no place for a vicar's son! As the Bishop said to the Actress.

One last memory of the Battery Charging Shop. Among the various workshops near to it was one which boasted an Alsation guard dog which, in travelling to and from B.C.S. duty, I got to know well enough to say "Hello!" and pat on the head. After an absence of a week or two when once again it was my turn on duty I was passing the dog and stretched out my right hand to pat it. My right arm was immediately seized in a vice-like grip and the dog was growling like mad. I had the sense to stand still and shout for help. Which help soon arrived from the workshop in the shape of an A/B corporal who shouted at the animal, cuffed it round the ear and sent it back into the workshop. Full of apologies he explained that the 'dog' had just had pups and was defending its litter. Point taken! It was a frightening moment which left me with a bruised arm, a respect for Alsations and an abiding memory.

M Section workshop was situated not far from the Parade Ground and it was here we did most of the repair work. It was rectangular in shape and one of a row of adjacent workshops. It had two windows above and to one side of the entrance door. Around the other three walls were work benches and very high shelves and a long workbench stood in the middle of the floor. From the many hours of routine duty spent in there only two outstanding memories remain.

Soldering was done by a copper-bit iron heated by a blow-lamp. Blow-lamps are 'primed' by pumping up the pressure and the resultant spray ignited by a lighted piece of material placed under the nozzle. On this particular occasion despite frantic pumping up the pressure, my blow-lamp failed to ignite. No spray coming out, therefore the nozzle must be blocked. There is a tool for such a contingency and I applied it. No sooner had I cleared the blockage than a huge jet of high pressured burning fuel shot forth. As I was on the middle work bench and the blow lamp was pointing at an angle of 45 degrees this parabolic flaming jet arced its way to the corner of the room, onto the shelf and set fire to pile of denims. I'd just invented the flame-thrower! Needless to say, it created quite a bit of fun and helped to relieve the monotony.

The other incident concerns the Pigeon Corps. Well, it wasn't really a Corp, but the 6th A/B Div. did have a Pigeon Unit - carrier pigeons. When all else fails, send up a pigeon? Anyhow, somebody one day decided that M Section should be taught how to handle a pigeon. The Instructor duly arrived at the workshop with his pigeons in the usual wicker basket and proceeded to give us a talk on pigeon handling, holding a pigeon in his hand and demonstrating as he talked. The lads from the North of England and particularly the mining fraternity were au fait with pigeons and pigeon crees and were, more or less, on familiar territory. For the rest it was a revelation. All went well until it came to the 'laying on of hands'. "Hold the bird gently but firmly", was the command and the bird was duly passed from hand to hand.

Somebody however must have squeezed the pigeon a bit too hard for we suddenly heard, "Aw, it's shit." Whoever he was then opened his 'sticky' hands thus releasing the struggling pigeon. It flew straight for the daylight and disappeared, flying like mad, across the Parade Ground. We were left almost in disbelief as we picked up the pieces of broken glass from the window through which it had had just smashed its way to freedom. Even Airborne pigeons were tough it seemed. Just to emphasise that statement, I heard the following tale. During an exercise on Salisbury Plain one of the parachuted canisters suffered a 'candle' i.e. the chute failed to open properly and was trailed above the canister looking for all the world like a big candle. The canister consequently crashed into the earth and was burst open. From the wreckage flew - an Airborne pigeon!!!

Finally, on D-Day when the Bridges over the Orne River and Canal were captured, besides radioing the message "Ham and Jam" to England signifying success, the news was also sent by carrier pigeon. The fact that it flew the wrong way initially made no difference as it did arrive in England. It has just occurred to me to wonder, could it have been one of the two whose stories I've just told? I'll never know!

Still in the Animal Kingdom, I remember one gloriously sunny day with time on my hands walking among the hills and fields near to Bulford Camp. I must have been broke otherwise I would have been in Salisbury. Anyhow, as I am enjoying the sun and the scenery, over the hill bounded a yellow labrador flinging what looked like an old glove up in the air. As it got closer I saw that the 'glove' was in fact a mole. Determined to save it, I got to it before the dog, after a fling, and picked it up. It was still very much alive and promptly tried to dig its way to freedom through the palms of my hands. I dropped it; the dog pounced and up in the air went the mole again. I grabbed it again when it landed but this time I used my beret. I found a large tuft of grass and, to save the mole and my beret through which it was trying to dig its way, I put the mole down by the tuft. Keeping the dog away I watched the mole dig like mad into the grass. Unable to do more I turned to continue my walk. I hadn't got far when I heard a shout. On turning round, the dog's owner had appeared on the scene and was calling for the dog. The dog was busy digging and my efforts at conservation were all in vain for up in the air once more sailed that poor mole. What eventually happened to the mole I've no idea but at least for a brief moment or two in its lifetime it was airborne and it had worn the red beret. Very few moles can say that!

The camp cinema was on the opposite side of the road to the rear of the guard room and was very well patronised and the film was changed twice during the week. I remember one night watching a Deanna Durbin and Franchot Tone film, 'His Butler's Sister', in which Deanna Durbin burst into tears, ran to her bedroom and flung herself on the bed. She was closely pursued by Franchot Tone who on seeing her lying sobbing on the bed opened his arms and said, "What do I do now?", and a large section of the audience told him! It was quite a while before the film could be heard again.

One night on guard duty the Sergeant got the tip-off that the duty officer was on the prowl. Taking the name of the Lord in vain he told me to get the prisoners back into their cells in double quick time.

"Where are they Sarge?", I asked.

"In the cinema", came the reply, "they're in the back row on the left."

Into the cinema I galloped and hissed to the back row on the left, "Duty officer on the prowl; get back quick", and three or four blokes shot out of their seats and beat me back to the guardroom.

I knew we looked after our own but that seemed ridiculous. Like the time I had to take one of the prisoners for exercise with strict orders not to lose him. We went up the road towards Beacon Hill and just as we reached the bottom of the hill he ran off the road and disappeared from view. I ran after him unslinging my rifle en route and discovered him sitting in a hollow of the field. "Put that bloody thing away", he said, "and give us a fag and come down here before some bugger sees you." I was so relieved I hadn't lost him I was happy to oblige.

Another example of how we looked after each other concerns a poor A/B bloke who was stopped by M.P.s at the barrier on Waterloo Station and was being booked for not having a pass. An A/B M.P. who was awaiting his turn to be checked at the barrier pushed forward and demanded to know what the trouble was. On being informed he said "Right, he's one of our lads, leave him to me and I'll sort the bastard out." Before the other M.P.s could protest he grabbed the lad took him through the barrier and proceeded to take his name, rank and number, and at the same time gave him a right telling off. Waiting until the other M.P.s' attention had been diverted by another 'customer', the A/B M.P. hissed, "Right, piss off! I haven't got a pass either." They then both went on their respective ways rejoicing.

It may sound as if discipline was lax in the Div. but not so, far from it. It was only when circumstances dictated and no one would suffer as a result the rules could be, and on occasion were, bent. Call it Airborne Initiative.

Netheravon airfield was just a few miles away and it was from there that we did glider training. We marched there and back of course so it was a relief to sit in a Hotspur glider and go for a ride. The Hotspur was very small and could only accommodate 6 or 7 bodies and even then we felt like sardines. I don't remember being scared on the first flight but I did urgently need a pee before climbing aboard and I relieved myself on the landing wheel and I wasn't alone. Having successfully landed after 'once round the airfield cabbie' it became a routine to pee on the landing wheel before every subsequent flight, operational flights included. It's strange how a superstition is formed and even stranger how you come to believe it.

When we graduated to Horsa gliders we also had to learn how to load them. In my case it was jeep and trailer and motorbike. Up the ramp, into the side of the glider, swing them round and lash them to the strong points with 'wire' ropes incorporating quick-release mechanisms. The glider pilots always had the last word as to positioning etc. We also learned to unload from the tail, down two steel U ramps. The only incident during training that stands out was one day when marching through the gates into Netheravon airfield some bright spark decided to liven up the proceedings by releasing gas - I blame the RAF but maybe it was our lot. Whomsoever; we had no gas masks with us and as it was the kind of gas which caused depression we were hurriedly stuffed into the Hotspurs and taken up into the wild blue yonder to breathe in God's pure air and recover from the suicidal tendencies of DN gas. Nevertheless it was a groggy lot that marched back to Bulford barracks that day.

Talking of peeing reminds me of a Corporal we had in our Barrack Room in the early Bulford days. He was a big chap with hands like frying pans and feet to match. A typical what used to be referred to as a farmer's boy - a B-I-I-I-G boy. Practical jokes were commonplace but the one he began to accuse us of playing on him was that of peeing on his bed. I say *on* as had it been *in* we could have blamed it on him as he was a very heavy drinker. No, it was on his bed, the proof being that his bed was occasionally soaked from the outside blankets through to his Biscuits (mattress).

The mystery was unbelievably and hilariously solved one night when a few of us returned late and, whilst getting ready for bed, saw this Corporal get out of bed. He then walked the length of the hut, totally ignoring us, went out of the hut and walked along outside the hut stopping at the windows opposite his bed. We stared in disbelief as he climbed through the window; stepped would be a better verb he was so big; walked over to his bed and proceeded to hose it down. About a pint and a half later he repeated his journey in reverse and climbed into his urine soaked 'pit'. The next morning, when we told him we knew who'd 'done it', among his many threatened revenges was one which we considered a physical impossibility but we said as the culprit was himself we'd be happy to watch! He took a lot of convincing but as there were so many witnesses he finally accepted the truth. Shortly afterwards he moved, to where we neither knew nor cared.

At some time or other we moved into a two-storey brick-built barracks and we occupied the top floor. It must have been some time in July - August because it was to that room I returned after going on leave to be married on September 4th. When I got back my bed space was empty and surveying the scene I observed my bed dangling from the rafters. One or two of the lads were sitting around on their beds enjoying the situation. I was tired, Sunderland to Bulford by train is a hell of a long journey and I must confess I didn't find the situation amusing. I then turned to my locker on the wall to start to start putting my kit away and there on the inside of the door when I opened it was stuck a rampant penis of green mottled soap. I wish I'd just laughed but I'm afraid I gave vent to my feelings by calling them all the bastards under the sun and flinging the offending "work of art" the length of the barrack room. At least I managed to get my bed down without breaking my neck.

We had a chap called Taffy Owens in our Section around this time who was an inveterate practical joker. Beds collapsed, bootlaces were tied to window handles, open a door and the roof fell in, he did it all, and what's more he did it all the time. Everybody was heartily sick of him and longed to get even but we could never catch him off guard - until one night! A few of us came back from Salisbury very late and found Taffy sound asleep look you! There was quite a discussion as to what to do including carrying his bed downstairs and leaving him in the middle of the parade ground - I believe that had actually happened to someone one time. Then I had a brilliant idea! "Just turn his bed round", I said and explained why! We all slept head to wall and feet to middle of room, and getting up to go to the toilet during the night you walked, half asleep and in the dark to the end of your bed and turned left or right depending which side you slept. Taffy got up in the small hours walked to the foot of his bed and walked straight into a brick wall. He was totally disorientated and went completely berserk, screaming his head off and pulling everybody out of bed and finished up sobbing with rage. It was a frightening performance but the practical joking stopped.

Training continued unabated and everyone was required to learn to drive. As I already held a licence courtesy of the GPO I was given the job of teaching a Scot called Archie. Until you've been a passenger in a jeep driven around the hedgerow lanes of Wiltshire by a wild-eyed almost petrified Scot who couldn't keep a straight line you've never lived. Not that the twisting, winding narrow lanes are straight but to have the jeep being bounced along the hedge and every few minutes being rammed into the foliage was very uncomfortable as well as damned dangerous.

Perseverance was eventually rewarded when Archie was pronounced qualified to drive. It was shortly afterwards that the Div. went on an artillery shoot to Sennybridge up in the Brecon Beacons. Lorries, jeeps pulling guns, jeeps pulling trailers and the odd staff car all in convoy from Bulford to Brecon. All went well until we got into the mountains and as we were going up an incline, mountains on one side and valley on the other, Archie changed into bottom gear. Well, that was his intention. What he actually did was change into reverse and start back down the slope scattering the convoy as he went. Jeeps, guns and trailers jack-knifed, some trying to climb up the mountain, others frantically trying to avoid going over the edge. Fortunately no one was hurt but by the time Archie had managed to stop, the convoy was a shambles.

Amongst the many catch-phrases that abounded in the forces then was the inevitable reply to any request you might make i.e. "Have you got a light?" - a fag - a hammer - an anything. The reply was always, "No! But I've got a sister in the WAAFs." It was a reply I could honestly make as my sister Elsie was in the WAAFs and was stationed near to Gloucester. Imagine my delight when, not only did our journey from Bulford to the Brecon Beacons pass close by the camp, but actually stopped in a large car park almost opposite. I've forgotten why we stopped, probably a meal break, but it gave me the opportunity to get permission to say a quick "Hello" to my sister.

Off I went and presented myself to the sentry on the gate and asked if I could see my sister. I was told to wait whilst permission was sought, via a telephone. Once given, she came to meet me and we spent a few minutes in animated conversation, indoors somewhere, glad to see each other. I was amused to learn from Elsie that she had been summoned to the phone and was asked, "Have you a brother in the Army?" To which she had replied in the affirmative. She was then asked, "What is his name?" She told them. Then came, "What coloured hat does he wear?" "He wears a red beret", said Elsie, who hadn't a clue what was going on. "He's at the gate, waiting to see you", gave her the answer. It was a wonderful moment and the only time we ever met 'In the field'. Then it was "Goodbye" and back on the road again en route to Wales.

This was in the winter of 1943 and the only reason I'm sure is because of the memory of the freezing conditions - or is it always winter in Sennybridge? One tiny stove in a barrack room is very little comfort even when it glows red-hot and you are almost on top of it. It doesn't help either when as you lift the lid to put in more coke some bloody idiot chucks in a handful of 9mm ammunition. I've never seen bodies move so fast, under beds, out of windows and through the door. What a noise! And how the hell the stove survived I don't know, but it did.

The other outstanding memory of Sennybridge was when I was grabbed by R.S.M. Carr and told I was to go to the top of the plateau on "look out".

"On the look out for what", I asked,

"German parachutists", said Carr grinning evilly.

It was night-time, it was dark and it was bloody freezing and there I am on top of the plateau with nothing between me and God except a biting, cutting wind. The ground was white with snow and I was shivering. To avoid freezing on the spot I kept on the move.

After about an hour of this I was wishing a German parachutist would appear to relieve the monotony. I was wishing anyone would appear or something would happen. When it did I wished it hadn't. I suddenly got a violent pain in the guts and I knew if I didn't get my pants off in double quick time I was going to be mighty uncomfortable. I dashed into a hedgerow and dropped them. My bum froze instantly except for the fundamental orifice from which, under high pressure, shot forth a scalding hot jet. The pain was awful and I suffered. Eventually my guts stopped boiling and something like normality returned. I discovered I had nothing in my pockets with which to clean myself and it was winter - there wasn't even a leaf on the hedge. There was only one thing left and I cleaned myself with handfuls of snow. It was the R.S.M. who came and told me to stand down and although I always thought I'd been set-up I couldn't think why and I never found out. One thing is certain however, I can never forget Sennybridge.

Chapter 6   Prelude to D-Day

From early 1944 to around early May things started to 'hot up'. We went on a twenty-five mile route march, full kit, including sten guns with which we had by now become proficient. The first part of the march was on the roadways. The second part was across country in a beeline for the camp. Whatever we encountered en route we went over, through or under. Quite a few of the lads suffered, we even took turns in helping to carry one back the last few miles, boots full of blood. Once on the Parade Ground the order was, "Boots and socks off and flat on your back, feet in the air." The M.O. made his inspection and quite a number had to have treatment for skinned toes, blisters etc. The poor bloke who we'd carried was hospitalised. I don't think he had any skin left on the soles of his feet.

There was also a three-day rifle shoot held. Out in the morning to the ranges, shooting all day at various targets and distances; application, rapid fire and snap shooting. We existed on jam and cheese sandwiches with a hot meal on return to barracks. When it was all over only two men of Div. Sigs. had qualified as marksmen, myself and Paddy Robertson. The results were so appalling that Div. Sigs. decided not to submit them to HQ and so although I'd qualified for a marksman's badge I didn't get one. Story of my life - qualified but lost out. What the Hell! I know I did it! After the results were announced the R.S.M. said "So you think you can shoot; I'll shoot you for a pound." With a very straight face I said I couldn't afford to risk a pound but I'd shoot him for nothing. I got away with it. He must have been in a good mood.

We also went on a scheme in the New Forest and although we didn't know it then, it was a rehearsal for D-Day. We had to get 'dug-in' and live on 24 hour ration packs which were housed in a waxed cardboard box about 9" x 7"x 4" containing six sheets of toilet paper, concentrated high vitamin chocolate, glucose sweets, tea, oatmeal & meat blocks and high protein biscuits. We had naphtha blocks and a small collapsible stand with which to heat meals but as these weren't very good we very soon resorted to using 'Benghazi' fires, biscuit tins filled with sand, doused in petrol and ventilation holes punched in the sides.

The town of Lewes wasn't far away and we managed the odd visit to sample the local brew. One pub crawl ended at a pub in which George Atkinson was involved in a game of darts with one of the locals. When we learned that George had still to get a double to start and the local only needed a double to win we gave him lots of encouragement like, "Pack it in George", "You'll never do it", "You haven't a chance".

George Atkinson, dart poised, phlegmatic Yorkshireman that he was answered, "I've seen these games won and I've seen them lost." After we'd seen him lose that one, it was pints all round but not on George. It was then that we decided to try the local Scrumpy for which I have had, ever since that night, a very healthy respect!!!

The favourite pastime of "Bill "Carter"" and "Ken "Harris"" was 'Cherchez la femme' with Bill doing most of the 'Cherchez-ing' and then involving Ken - not that the latter had any objections. Well, he did have one which we often heard and that was that he didn't know where Bill found his women because they were a lot of old bags! Eventually Ken said that he'd had enough and for Bill to keep his women for himself. We heard no more from Ken for a while until one day he regaled us with a sad little tale. It appeared that while on this scheme in the New Forest Bill came to Ken full of excitement and said he'd found a smasher and that she had a friend who was just right for Ken. Ken took a lot of persuading but eventually agreed to go with him to meet them. He continued "When we got to this little thatched cottage Bill knocked on the door and it was opened by a real smasher, about 17, blonde with blue eyes and big tits and I thought, he's done it, he's got a real smasher at last. And then the bastard said, 'Is your Granny in?'." Bill never lived it down and a new catch phrase was born.

We all lived as one unit but actually belonged to different Sections. I remember H, J, K, L & M Sections. J, K and L. were Parachute attached, H was Royal Artillery attached and M, the general maintenance section for all, was the one I originally belonged to. By the time 1944 arrived I had been posted to H Section. Reading the noticeboard one day I saw they were asking for volunteers to join J Section and take a parachute course. I didn't seem to be getting anywhere and decided to change course and have a shot at it. Another of the lads feeling the same way decided to join me so off we set. En route for Company Office to volunteer for J Section I suddenly and inexplicably stopped and said "No! It's not for me" and returned to barracks, and to H Section for the rest of my service. There was no voice, no blinding light, no premonition, it happened just as I said. I was to hear much later on that the lad who volunteered instead of me was killed on landing on D-Day.

Sometime about now Div. Sigs asked for volunteers to act as French interpreters, D-Day was obviously looming, applicants to be interviewed by Major 'Lucky' Fenton. Fancying my chances with my schoolboy French I duly turned up at Company Office. There was a queue of about half a dozen waiting. Eventually in I went. Major Fenton was seated at his desk and he barked out a string of incomprehensible (well it was to me) French Canadian patois, which I believe was his mother tongue.

"Pardon?" I said.

"NEXT!" he shouted.

Well, I tried!

We had a Sergeant Ogle who pre-dated Mr. Magoo and was so short sighted I'm sure he could not see past the headlamp of his motorbike. I was in Company Office one day with a few of the lads when in came Sergeant Ogle and said to George Atkinson "Have you seen George Atkinson?"

"Yes", replied George, "He's just gone across the Parade Ground."

"Thanks", said Ogle, and went out to look for him.

Speaking of motorbikes. Sgt. 'Legs' Gummit spent a lot of time racing about on his bike from Bulford to Amesbury Abbey which was Div. HQ. The gates at Amesbury Abbey, wrought iron I believe, were always open and 'Legs' would roar round the corner, through the gateway and up the drive. One night, one very dark night, somebody took it into his head to shut the gates. Habit dies hard and 'Legs' roared round the corner and - finished up in hospital.

He was to be hospitalised again due to another smash on his bike. This time it was in Normandy, some time after D-day. Whilst he was recuperating someone asked him what happened. "Well", he said, "I was coming along this road one night and coming towards me were two small lights about two yards apart. I thought, two Frenchmen on bicycles, I'll scare the hell out of them! So I roared between the two of them and hit a Bren carrier!!!"

One rainy day we were marched out into the rolling Salisbury Plain and, in a large hollow, formed three sides of a square. There we stood, at ease, getting thoroughly soaked through, for a very long time indeed. Eventually the rain eased and over the hill came a jeep which made its way to the fourth side of our square and stopped. By now we could see our expected VIP. Montgomery got out of the jeep, climbed onto the bonnet and said, "Gather round." He then proceeded to give us a pep talk the gist of which was that very soon we were going to hit the Germans for six, we were a great bunch of blokes and he had every confidence in us etc. and he wished us all good luck. We were brought to attention and off he went. Highly elated and highly saturated we squelched our way back to Bulford. It had been a good show.

Not so, however, when we were introduced to the Boyes Anti-Tank Rifle. It was a brute of a gun firing large calibre bullets, small shells. The recoil was such that even with both legs straight out and toes dug into the ground as was recommended you were still well and truly hammered back. Our target was an old tank about 300 yards away and we were given 2 clips of 5 rounds and then the order rapid fire. I banged away merrily, got through one clip loaded and started on the second clip. The noise was deafening, so much so that I didn't know that the R.S.M. was trying to attract my attention until he started kicking my boots. My ears were ringing so much that I had difficulty in hearing him but as he was in a bit of a rage and shouting his head off I got the message.

"Who the hell told you to fire the second clip?"

"Wasn't the order rapid fire?" I asked. "Nobody said 5 rounds rapid fire"

A moments pause while he thought and then, "Huh! you're right", and he walked away down the line of prone but very interested bodies!

That night I couldn't sleep, being driven mad by the ringing in my ears which I had obviously damaged. The constant ringing persisted and I was being driven frantic and I reported sick. I was eventually sent to a specialist who happened to be a woman. After various questions and tests, a stainless steel tube was pushed up my nose and turned towards my eardrum. A rubber tube and bulb was then attached and air pumped towards my eardrum, from the inside. It was painful! I suppose she was trying to free something or other.

At the end of the torture she asked me if there was any improvement and I answered quite truthfully, yes, I could hear the ringing much better now. She didn't like that one bit and in a roundabout way practically accused me of trying to 'work my ticket' i.e. get my discharge from the army because of the pending Invasion. I couldn't have been more insulted and said so and finally convinced her of the truth - all I wanted was to stop the ringing in my ears. She told me nothing more could be done and the problem might clear up in a day or two, a week or two, a month or two, or probably never. The latter proved correct! 50 years on I still suffer with tinitus and only in 1995, at the urging of my family, applied for and received a small pension, but sadly, not retrospective.

Weekend passes could be obtained fairly frequently, 36 hours being the usual time allowed. To reach Sunderland and return in that time was pretty difficult and considering the time spent at home hardly worth the trouble or expense. It became the norm to acquire your pass not at 12 noon on the Saturday, but as soon after tea on the Friday and then take a chance you wouldn't be missed and buzz off. That gave me most of Saturday at home and a bit of Sunday before having to be back for first parade Monday morning. In actual fact it should have been midnight Sunday but - many a night was spent on Salisbury Station waiting for the milk train or equivalent.

Early May 1944 the whole Div. was given leave and a few of us 'wangled' our passes as usual and went off camp to the main road to await the bus to the Station. Just as we were boarding the bus George Atkinson appeared from the camp area waving frantically. He was obviously trying to call us back, but why and for what we neither knew nor cared, the bit was between our teeth, so we waved him goodbye and off we went. We should have got off the bus and I wish we had. What had happened was that, as always, the army was going to organise the mass leave by numbers. Those furthest away i.e. Scotland, Hebrides, Ireland etc. would leave around 10:00 on Saturday, those in the North East, Midlands, Wales would leave an hour later, the rest at noon. The army was providing transport to the stations and trains had been allocated. Everybody had to be seen to board the lorries and ticked off the lists. The man responsible for the lists was the Company Office Clerk and he found out we'd got our passes and were going. That evening, Friday, he told George if he didn't stop us he would have to report us. George didn't, he did.

We all got a telegram ordering us back to Bulford a day before our leave was due to expire. We were put on a charge, got 14 days jankers and lost a days pay. My punishment, apart from extra drill, was weeding the Sergeants' Mess Garden and I think I got off lightly. Even then it only lasted 5 days before the Div. moved into a transit camp. We moved by road taking everything with us and going through villages people came out of their houses to give us cups of tea and cakes.

They knew and we knew that D-Day wasn't far off. They waved, smiled, shook hands and wished us well and 'God blessed' us and some of us 'mother's bairns' got a kiss. We were totally enveloped in goodwill and we went to our barb-wired, strict security transit camp and were sealed in, incommunicado, for the next fortnight, or maybe just ten days, I forget. The time was spent in cleaning and checking weapons, and being briefed: sand maps, photographs and very detailed info. regarding our objectives was vouchsafed and finally we were told our destination: Ranville, Normandy.

In between times while all this was taking place we had a lot of leisure time which was spent mostly playing cards. Somebody had the bright idea of paying us in sixpences and as we had stocked up with cigarettes and had nowhere to go except the NAFFI and spend our money we played pontoon. Money was going to be no good to us, so it was sixpence a card at least and I can still see the pile of sixpences in the middle of the tent floor. We were issued with 'Mae Wests' and two screw on gas bottles to inflate each wing as and when required. The gas bottles came in stout cardboard boxes which came in very handy for storing cigarettes. I think I must have had about 200, cigarettes not boxes.

We were also issued with some very interesting items to whit; silk maps, rubber encased hacksaw blade and two metal shirt buttons which when inverted and balanced one on the other made a compass with a tiny dot of paint on one of them to indicate North. All of which was to aid escape if captured. We also got a small tin box housing two small bottles of water purifying tablets and rather ominously a sealed tin holding a 'tubunic ampoule' of morphine. We were also issued with little 3" square, newly minted, French Franc notes. Why? I never found out. We certainly weren't going on a shopping expedition. Bribery to aid escape perhaps. All those items survive with the exception of the silk maps and shirt buttons.

We had been hanging around in the camp for so long it was decided to bring in a film unit to entertain us. It was then discovered that in the double marquee which was to serve as the cinema there was no power supply. Sergeant Bowkett rose to the occasion, as he was to do many times in the future, and said "Leave it me, Sah." He then grabbed me after having explained the job and said, "Right bloke, fix it." Me. Why me? I was nearest I suppose!

Electricity was supplied to the camp and carried on poles via two insulated wires, to the various Admin. points. The cables ran past the marquee so it seemed a good idea to remove an inch of insulation from each leg and attach a "drop-in" to the marquee. This I duly did, breaking God knows how many safety regulations, and ran the cable into the marquee down one of the supporting poles to which I taped a socket and hoped it would work. The great moment arrived later on when the film was shown. It was Lena Horne in 'Stormy Weather' - shades of the C.L.B. and Blyth! Although at that time it was sweltering hot it proved to be a very prophetic title as it was due to stormy weather that D-Day was postponed. We had duly loaded the gliders and got on board at Tarrant Rushton airfield on June 4th but were stood down for 24 hours.

As the airfield had loads of indigenous chalk lying around, many of the Horsas were daubed with messages and slogans. On mine I wrote in block capitals my wife's name 'ENA' just under the pilot's cockpit. On the front I wrote 'LILLIBULERO'. As that was the signature tune of a then current radio programme called 'Into Battle' I thought it very appropriate. Most of the time of course we listened to the 'This is the American Forces Network'.

I am reminded of the only other time I wrote, well actually painted, my wife's name on anything else. It was on my 2-stroke motorbike. I painted 'Ena' on the petrol tank and left it to dry. When I returned it had been changed to 'Black Enamel', but once again I digress.

Back to the airfield where, on June 5th, I duly peed on the glider wheel again before climbing on board and settling down for the off. We were in full gear, flying smock, helmet, belt, webbing, full ammunition pouches (Sten 9 mm), sten gun, small and big pack, water bottle, entrenching tool and Mae West. Instead of being highly blancoed and polished however it was all painted black and green with faces to match. Tucked inside my smock were my two boxes of cigarettes.

 # 8   Invasion currency issued in May 1944

Chapter 7　　　　Destination: Ranville

We were assembled in serried ranks and towed by Halifax bombers The takeoff was smooth. Once airborne we relaxed, undid our webbing, took out our enamel mugs, opened up the A/B flasks and had a cuppa, smoked and chatted. I was on the port side at the front, one of about eight I think. Behind us was my fully loaded jeep and trailer and a motor bike. There we sat being towed across the Channel en route to God knows what.

It was a bit bumpy at one point but worse was to come. The doors to the cockpit were open and in the moonlight we were able to see the towing plane and where we were going, which was all very interesting. Suddenly somebody said "Cor! Look at that" and there in the distance we could see a very pretty firework display. Coloured lights slowly moving up in parabolic arcs, dozens of them. By now we were all standing up crowding through the doors trying to get a good look. The glider pilots yelled at us to get back and strap up. What we were looking at was flak and tracer and we weren't helping the trim of the glider. We needed no second telling. The pilots closed the doors.

It must have been nearly 3 a.m. when we reached the French Coast and the flak. Tension was pretty high by now and all chatter had stopped. It was then that an R.A. officer sitting to my right undid his safety harness, stood up and took off his helmet which he then placed upside down on the seat and sat on it. There he sat, hanging grimly on to his safety harness rolling about as the glider 'bumped' its way through the exploding shells. We watched him in silent bewilderment and then someone asked the question which I'm sure we were all thinking, "Excuse me Sir, but why did you do that?"

With an absolutely straight face he replied, "Well, I don't know about you chaps, but I hope to get married someday when we get back to England, and I'm not about to have my bloody chances ruined." We exploded with laughter and the tension broke and once over the coast and through the flak we were fairly relaxed as we flew on to our destination.

Once we had cast off and the noise of the four-engined Halifax had gone the silence was uncanny as the glider pilot circled and lost height seeking a landing spot. Having found one the glider went into a steep dive at around 90 m.p.h. and almost at the last moment pulled out and flattened out preparatory to landing. We were committed now and if there happened to be a pole, a wall, a ditch, a hedge, a building or another glider en route it was just hard lines.

There was a thump as the pilot levelled out to land and it was at that moment that I did something very stupid. I pulled the quick release pin, undid my harness, stood up and started to make my way to the front exit. I was going to be first out. The next moment the wheels underneath the Horsa hit the ground, checked its speed considerably, and I was catapulted forward headfirst into the door leading to the cockpit. Thank God for steel helmets! Even so, I could have broken my neck.

We juddered finally to a halt with a couple more jarring thumps. I think we must have hit anti-landing poles, 'Rommel's Asparagus' as they became known, and then there we were safe and sound on a field in the Landing Zone North of Ranville. As things turned out I was last out, the others having exited around and over me as I lay on the floor!

9   Two Horsas in the fields North of Ranville 10/06/1944

Photograph courtesy of the Imperial War Museum, London (BU2426)

The nearest glider has landed with its undercarriage intact and the port-side exit door remains several feet above ground level. The rear unloading ramp is in place.

The exit at the front of a Horsa must be about 5 feet from ground level and as I stood looking down I could just see the ground in the clouded moonlight. I jumped, braced myself to hit the ground and hit - nothing. Nothing until two or three feet lower down when I finally hit the ground with a resounding thump and, for the second time in a few minutes, found myself sprawling in a heap. We had landed in a cornfield and I had mistaken the top of the corn for ground level.

I must now explain that whilst being briefed, various units had been given various challenge and reply code words just in case you needed to distinguish friend from foe. Words such as "Laurel" which required "Hardy" as an answer, "knife" and "fork", "fish" and "chips" etc. I don't think anyone had considered that in the chaos of a night-time A/B landing we might get mixed up. We did. Some of us didn't even land in the right place. As I picked myself up from the ground an officer came creeping round the front of my glider, stuck a revolver, still attached to the lanyard, in my face and hissed, "Laurel."

I've got all my equipment on, flying smock, helmet and all, I couldn't have been anything other than what I was and here I am being 'Laurel'ed'. It was like a scene from one of their films and I couldn't help grinning as I replied, "It's all right Sir, I'm on your side - but I think I'm 'Fish and Chips'!"

"Take care", he said and disappeared.

The first priority was to unload the glider to which end the lads had pulled the 'quick release' pins holding the bolts which held the tail section on. It should have dropped off but it didn't! All efforts to dislodge it failed, the tail section held firm and so did the jeep, trailer and motorbike. There then followed 'Laurel and Hardy Take 2'.

The lads started jumping up and down on the floor in the tail in an effort to dislodge it. The equivalent of sitting on a tree limb and sawing yourself off. Fortunately that didn't work or we would have had a few casualties. Someone then turned up with a rope which was duly tied round the tail and then it was "heave, heave" to no avail. In the meantime someone else had a brainwave, There was in the glider a stainless steel axe with an insulated handle to be used for emergencies i.e. hacking your way out of a crashed landing. For the next 'God knows how long' we took it in shifts to 'hack and heave' and, despite being told before we left England not to make a noise on landing, there we were sitting on top of and around the tail end of a Horsa glider, hacking and heaving and making one helluva noise!!!

While this was going on I was grabbed by someone to help him remove a body from his glider. It was a battery Sergeant Major who'd apparently broken his neck on landing. I took his legs and the other chap took his arms and I remember his head bumping on the duckboards as we took him out. I didn't think that was right and I said, "Lift him up a bit his head's bumping the floor"

To which came the reply, "He can't feel it." We laid him in the hedge and then came the remark, "I wish I had a couple of pins." When I asked why I discovered he'd been an undertakers assistant in Civvy Street, and he said he used pins to keep eyes closed. I left them both and went back to my glider.

By now a small bulldozer had appeared and attaching a steel hawser to the tail tried to haul it off. The steel hawser simply ripped though the plywood and we were no better off. Along came an officer and grabbed some of us to help move a glider which had landed across the only road from the L.Z. despite another directive when being briefed, "... and don't block the roads!" It was eventually moved by the bulldozer. When I got back to my glider, the tail had given up the struggle and had finally dropped off and had blocked the exit. We had to shift it before we could get the cargo out. Easier said than done. A Horsa tail section is a helluva size and there isn't anything you can really get hold of. Rock it, yes. Move it, no way.

Our landing had been unopposed despite sounds of distant gunfire but now came the CRUMP, CRUMP, CRUMP, of mortar shells landing somewhere near. It's marvellous what you can do when the adrenalin flows and, like leaping a five-bar gate when chased by a bull, we picked that tail up and dumped it in the hedge side, got the jeep, trailer and bike unloaded and set off for our rendezvous.

 # 10   Horsas in the fields near Ranville 15/06/1944

Photograph courtesy of the Imperial War Museum, London (B5593)

The fuselage and tail section of the nearest Horsa show matching damage possibly caused by attempts to free the retaining bolts. The nose wheel of the glider beyond has collapsed on landing and the port-side exit door is only just above ground level.

On the way across the channel instead of going to the trouble of repacking our mugs after finishing drinking tea we just hung them on the straps of our packs. Now here we were walking almost waist high through the cornfield, in single file, a white enamel mug gleaming in the moonlight on our backpacks. I couldn't help thinking, "a fat lot of good our camouflage is now." However I soon had something else to occupy my mind. Coming out of the cornfield onto open ground I saw a bren gun, fully loaded. I expect it had been 'lost' or jettisoned by one of the Paras earlier on. Happy to swell my armoury I picked it up rejoicing in my good luck and went on to Ranville village which was just down the road.

The Chateau was to be Div. HQ and now that we'd arrived with General 'Windy' Gale so it was. Someone, I forget who, told me to dig in "there". "There" was behind the Chateau at the edge of a clump of trees and beyond were two fields and an old farm. One of the fields had an old pump right in the middle and I remembered yet another directive we'd been given - "don't drink the local water!"

Preparatory to digging I discovered that the quick release pin from my harness was still dangling from my right hand middle finger. I tucked it into my smock and subsequently it became one of my souvenirs.

I'd just got started to dig when what sounded like an angry hornet snarled past my right ear, a leaf flew off the nearby bushes, and then I heard the crack of a rifle in the distance. I weighed about $8½$ stone in those days and I wasted no time in trying to stuff it all into the 6 inch depression I'd so far managed to dig. As I did so I was very much aware that I'd been singled out by a sniper and that my war, barely three hours old, had suddenly become very personal.

My thoughts were interrupted by a couple of Paras who came crouching through the bushes and said, "Where did that shot come from?"

I chanced raising an arm and pointed saying, "Over there."

I didn't need any telling but nevertheless they said, "Keep down", and sped off. A few minutes later there came a few bursts of Bren gun fire and they were nice enough to return and tell me, "He won't bother you again." I was delighted to hear it and set to with renewed vigour to dig myself a slit trench.

There were no immediate repairs to do and no batteries to charge but even if there had been it wouldn't have mattered because everybody was 'stood to'. From landing at 3 a.m. on the 6th until the morning of the 8th everyone was 'stood to' in a defensive attitude around Div. HQ. My post was under some trees looking out across a narrow lane that ran down one side of the chateau grounds. Beyond the lane was a field and beyond the field was a wood and that was where the counter attack was expected. I had my Sten and about a dozen magazines, I had a couple of '36' grenades but most important of all I had the Bren I'd picked up. I reckoned on giving a good account of myself when the time came.

Hardly anyone slept on the 4th when the invasion was postponed and no one slept on the 5th and now it was the 6th and then the 7th. I had my water bottle and sweets, biscuits and chocolate from the 24-hour ration pack but no chance as yet to cook. By the night of the 7th I was bleary eyed and I began to hallucinate. In the dark I began to see Germans rising from the grass in the field opposite and coming towards me. A shake of the head did wonders plus a good talking to, from myself of course. What really saved the day though was that it rained and rained, and that woke me up. It also soaked me despite the shelter of the trees. I have often wondered how I managed to stay awake so long.

Next morning, the 8th, we stood down and the first job was to clean our weapons. When I stripped the Bren gun my blood ran cold. It had no firing pin!!! Somewhere from the dim and distant past I could now hear a voice saying, "...and if you have to jettison your weapons make sure 'Jerry' can't use them."

By now the bridges over the Orne Canal and River had been captured, Ranville and Benouville taken, Merville batteries silenced, and the Commandos and other troops had linked up with us. The Germans now knew they had an invasion on their hands, counter attacks were being launched and we came under ever increasing mortar and shell fire. On the 9th everybody was on 'stand to' again and out in the fields surrounding Div. HQ. I now had plastic explosive which I wrapped around my grenades. It's strange the things you think about waiting to be attacked. I had my grenades and ammo in the bottom of the slit trench and I thought - "If a mortar bomb lands in here that lot won't help matters" - so I laid them on the ground in front of me. Then I thought, "If that lot's hit by a bullet I'll probably get my head blown off" - so I put them back in the slit trench and reasoned, "What the hell, if a shell lands in here I've had it anyway."

While still thinking about it, Lt. Gladwyn hove into view and told me to take a message to someone on the far side of the field. I think it was to report to him as soon as we 'stood down'. Me? Why me? As I ran over towards the woods on the other side of the field I felt completely naked. I was certainly the only silly B above ground and therefore exposed. Message duly delivered I got back to my slit trench in double quick time and settled down again amongst my grenades and ammo and oddly enough felt much safer.

The expected attack duly arrived but was beaten back and contained by the Paras who knocked out two tanks a couple of fields away and eventually we all got back to doing our jobs. Shelling and mortaring make life extremely difficult and with slit trenches all over the Chateau grounds it wasn't uncommon for more than one body to dive into one as and when circumstances dictated.

By now we all had lids on the slit trenches as Jerry was using air bursts and mortar shells were exploding among tree branches. It was during one of these bombardments that Ted Cooper and two or three others dived into one hole and shut the 'lid'. In time breathing became difficult and someone was so claustrophobic that he wanted the lid opened. Nobody else did, and I don't blame them.

"For Christ's sake open the lid", came the plea.

Various replies, all ending in "off", followed.

" I can't breathe – open the effing lid", once again came the frantic plea.

The situation was becoming unbearable but as the bombardment was still going on no way was the lid going to be opened. However as our claustrophobic friend was becoming desperate it was decided to relieve the situation by poking a 'breathing hole' through the lid with a bayonet, which was duly done.

Almost immediately Ted Cooper shouted, "I've been hit!"

Various replies followed like, "Don't be so effing stupid", "Stop being daft", "How the hell can that happen?"

"I tell you I've been hit!", said Ted – and so he had! A piece of shrapnel had whizzed through the 'breathing hole' and buried itself in his leg!

Ted had got what in my Father's day was called a 'Blighty' and that was where he finished up in double quick time. All casualties were flown back to England. Sometime later, back in England, my wife observed through the front window of 2 Grange Terrace, Grangetown, Sunderland (her Mother's home and ours pro temp) an A/B Signals soldier in hospital blue and red beret waiting at the bus stop for a bus to Ryhope Military Hospital and she thought, "I wonder?"

On enquiring if he had come from Normandy and being told "Yes" the next question was "I wonder if you know my husband Ted Hold?" He was able to tell her I'd landed O.K. and I was O.K. when he left me. Ted Cooper could have been sent anywhere in England, but outside our front door? Remarkable coincidence or fate? I just don't know.

To return to the Chateau. I had a shallow trench excavated to protect the batteries and the chore horse with which I charged them and I had a camouflaged parachute silk awning draped over them from the bushes to the ground. Lots of used parachutes around, in fact we made use of them to line our slit trenches and as protection against the cold at night. I even managed to bring one home which was used to make undies I think. Anyhow, here I am taking specific gravity readings underneath the awning when BRAFF, BRAFF, BRAFF it started to rain mortar shells. Too late to run anywhere, I'm caught in the open and all I can do is go flat which I promptly did alongside the batteries. Later on that same day I am back in exactly the same spot doing exactly the same thing when I noticed on my hands and arms shafts of sunlight. On looking up I saw the awning was full of holes, shrapnel holes! I sat there for quite a while trying to work out how I hadn't been hit. As there had been no further attack since I was last attending to my job I knew those holes had been made at that time - and I was underneath! I think I decided it was all due to the angle of entry and in any case I'd been lucky - again!

It was around about now that Div. HQ decided to improve their lighting system by salvaging the lights and batteries from the gliders on the LZ and I was given the job. As the Germans had been massing in that area and it had been duly shelled it was suggested I take great care and not hang around too long as there might be a few of them still active - but the lights and batteries were needed, so -. Sergeant Bowkett, who had of course, I am sure, volunteered me for the job, came with me and we set to keeping a wary eye and ear open for trouble. The batteries were housed in the cockpits and the lights were at the centre of the glider.

It was exhausting work but we managed to salvage quite a lot and loaded the jeep with about twelve sets. I'd even had a brainwave, the cigarettes which I'd so carefully packed and stuffed in my smock were missing when I first got to the Chateau after landing. They had obviously dropped in the glider after undoing my webbing and standing up - I would now retrieve them! What a hope - at least I retrieved my own light and subsequently lit my own dug-out. I was also very interested to observe the perfect circular dent I had made in the plywood cockpit door with my head on landing.

During our wandering round the LZ going from glider to glider we did see the odd German or two but being dead they were no bother. One of them I thought might still be alive as he was in a kneeling position with his back towards me, but when I approached him from the other side he was well and truly dead his face contorted with agony as he held his ripped open guts with both hands. Livestock and particularly horses were also casualties of war and the unmistakable smell of death was to permeate everything in the months that followed.

Div. HQ suffered a great deal of bombardment on a daily basis and continued to do so. Battery charging and repairs became a regular routine. Damage was mostly due to 'snatch-plugs' becoming disconnected due to misuse i.e. cables being pulled apart instead of being 'broken' properly. The 'snatch-plugs' then had to be opened up and wires resoldered. Solid copper soldering irons heated by blowlamp was the best we could do in the field. Radio valves could be changed and transmitter's insets changed when necessary. Anything more complicated had to go to M Section who had a small workshop set up. Petrol driven 'chore horses' had long exhausts which were buried in the ground, with the exception of the end, to minimise noise. It was round the clock maintenance grabbing meals and sleep as you could, and in between keeping your 'head down; speaking of which -

"Right bloke, bring the jeep and your gear"

"Where are we going Sarge?"

"I'll show you."

It turned out to be another of Sergeant Bowkett's 'voluntary' efforts, this time in a field some way up the road in which one of the Para brigades was engaged in action with the enemy. Their radio was on the blink and here I am flat on my belly trying to diagnose the trouble and fix it. The ground rose slightly in front and shifting my position to get a better look at the problem I raised my head above the rise.

I was promptly flattened by one of the Paras who yelled above the din "Keep your bloody head down, do you want to finish up like them?", nodding his head in the direction of somewhere behind me. I turned my head and found myself looking at about half a dozen bodies covered with blankets. I changed a couple of valves and we left.

On another occasion I went off on my own to change some batteries at one of the forward units and managed to take the wrong road on the return journey. I'd been travelling for a while and was wondering why Ranville and Div. HQ hadn't yet appeared on the horizon when I was brought to an abrupt halt by a couple of Paras who jumped out of the ditch and waved me down.

"Where the hell do you think you're going?"

"Div. HQ", I said.

"Oh! no you're not" he said. "Jerry's up that bloody road, Div. HQ's behind you." As if to confirm this statement Jerry obligingly opened up. The Paras dived back in the ditch and I did the fastest U-turn of my life and went hell for leather in the opposite direction.

I came into Ranville from an unfamiliar direction and stopped to get my bearings. I also lit a cigarette to get my breath back, contradictory as that may seem. On my left, among some trees, was another jeep and a group of officers in deep discussion. One of them looked over and said to me,

"Where are you going soldier?"

"Div. HQ, Sir", I said slinging him a salute. "Can you tell me where it is please?"

"Just round the corner", he said and followed that with, "You're doing a good job so don't spoil it by smoking while you're driving."

"No Sir, Thank you Sir", I said and drove off realising I'd just been nicely bollicked by Lieutenant Colonel Smallman-Tew, O.C. of the 6th A/B Div. Sigs. Although with so much shot and shell flying around I couldn't help wondering what further damage a cigarette could add.

Chapter 8   Entrenched in Ecarde

The Germans had excellent radio and direction finding equipment and I feel sure that helped them to pinpoint Div. HQ to the extreme that we came in for a lot of attention. I don't know if that was the reason Div. HQ moved but in any case we did, to a place called Ecarde, on the 25th June. North of Ranville there is a road leading to Sallenelles and about a mile along this road a narrow track leads down a steep slope past some large houses and turns right along the foot of an escarpment into which have been driven two or three quarries. This track runs almost parallel to the Orne canal and is separated from it by about three fields. It was into these fields that we dug in and made it home from home for the next two months or so. I was to travel along that track many times and found it very touching that on the corner where it joined the Sallenelles road was a grave marked by a wooden stave and helmet, on which were placed fresh wild flowers. No matter how many times I passed it the flowers were fresh and although I never saw any civilians I think it must have been them who tended the grave.

The field I was in rose slightly from the quarry side and I chose the top left hand corner in which to dig and promptly found a rubbish dump. Fortunately it was only a small dump and I dug down about four or five feet, put a roof over the top with just enough room to get in and out. During the weeks which followed I made it more habitable with shelves and recesses dug out of the sides and of course, a light fastened onto the roof. My charging was done in the open field behind me, exhaust once again buried to minimise the noise. It didn't take the Germans long to find us again and the mortaring and shelling continued.

There was one particular night when the shelling was very fierce and when it had stopped a wild-eyed figure dived into my slit trench shouting, "They've sunk the Navy, they've sunk the Navy." It was Archie of Sennybridge fame and when I'd managed to calm him down I got the story. Off shore was the Royal Navy providing shell fire as, when and where needed, and highly effective it was too. Radio communication shore to ship was provided by a Royal Navy Forward Observation Unit who relayed map references and fire orders as the occasion demanded. The Navy F.O.U. had a dug out beside us and it had been hit, hence Archie and "They've sunk the Navy."

Not long after moving to Ecarde the weather changed and it rained long and hard. Some of the lads had dug communicating trenches from one slit trench to the other and as the field had a slight rise the slit trenches filled up and flowed from one to the other and washed then all out. I'm O.K. in the top left hand corner - damp, yes, but intact.

Walking one day along the dirt track by the quarry in the soaking rain I could hear a motor bike coming down the slope around the corner and I stopped and moved to one side to wait until it had got past. Round the corner it came, skidded and deposited its rider face down in the mud. His back was towards me as he rose and wiping the mud from his face he cursed the weather, the bike and the war. Turning to pick up his bike he saw me, standing as I was in open-mouthed admiration, and said "Filthy weather isn't it?" Kick starting his bike the padre shot off down the path. Somehow after that, the weather didn't seem all that bad.

M Section had set up a workshop three or four fields away and I had a No. 19 radio transmitter/receiver set which needed their attention so off I went. I was very, very tired, the 19 set was quite heavy and as I was ducking through a barbed wire fence I managed to snag my left forearm and rip it open. When I got back the C.O. spotted me and asked what had happened and I said it was O.K. it was only barbed wire. He insisted I go to the Medical Centre in the village. A new group of medics had just arrived on the scene, I think they were Dutch. They hadn't even had time to unpack their lorry and I was their first customer. I was made quite a fuss of and came back well and truly bandaged up. I still have the scar and as it was the only injury I was to suffer I consider myself extremely lucky.

On another similar occasion the outcome was somewhat different. This time I wasn't tired, I was exhausted, a walking Zombie. When I staggered into M Section field carrying yet another 19 set one of the lads said "My God you look terrible, sit down there (a tree trunk) and I'll get you a drink." He came back with a mug two thirds full of water and I downed it gratefully in one gulp. He stood there in wide-eyed amazement as I did so and in two seconds I knew why. I couldn't get my breath, my eyes filled up and my ears popped.

I finally managed to gasp, "What the hell was that?" It was my first introduction to Calvados - and raw Calvados at that! It did wonders for my exhaustion and in a very short space of time I was ready to take on the entire German army single handed.

The rain which persisted for some time brought problems with the radio sets which of course got soaked and rendered them unserviceable. Using the exhaust of the chore horse as a drying agent proved very successful and helped greatly to keep communications open. Transmitter insets being carbon-granules type were also U/S (unserviceavble) when wet and they too could be dried out but prevention being better than cure an ingenious idea was born. Oddly enough by something used to prevent birth, Durex. With care, a transmitter insert could be wrapped in a Durex and replaced in the transmitter mouthpiece. Sound got through O.K. but not water. Care had to be taken however when screwing the mouthpiece on so as not to rupture the Durex. During the rainy weather I made sure I had my pockets full of Durex.

Once we got established at Ecarde a rudimentary field kitchen materialised, COMPO rations (tinned food) turned up and we could now have a real hot meal. It was usually stew of one sort or another and half a slice of plum duff - no custard. The last of the Div. who had travelled by sea joined us and Derek Hogarth having seen the wreckage of war and particularly the gliders was amazed but pleased to find us still alive - we of course shared his pleasure. Derek joined me in my dug out even going to the extent of making a small notice board "THE MAQUIS" for the entrance to 'chez nous' and I added a pair of clogs salvaged from a cobblers shop in Colombelle which had been hit and I still have them.

Sergeant Bowkett managed to volunteer me three more times for jobs which I still consider as extra curricular! The first was to a field near Breville for which there had been a terrific ding-dong battle and which as a result was virtually destroyed. He took me to a Sherman tank which was dug in, being used as artillery, and had a 19 set on the blink. Two lads had an awning over a big open dug out behind the tank and to my surprise they had a young French girl with them. She was just a kid, perhaps 12 or 13, but very pretty and I was able to converse with her. She was all alone, home and family gone and these two lads had taken her under their wing. From her broken English they had also taught her to swear which they thought was very funny. The poor kid didn't know of course what she was saying. I managed however to tell her in my schoolboy French that the words were bad and not at all lady-like. I often wonder what became of her.

Bowkett's next effort was a snorter.

"Right bloke, get your gear, bring the jeep."

"Where are we going Sarge?"

"I'll show you", said Bowkett and off we went into the Normandy fields not far from Ecarde. Eventually we turned off a road into a field in the corner of which was a little Auster, an army spotting plane.

"Right! Over there", said Bowkett and I duly drove over to the plane and stopped. By this time I'm wondering what an army spotting plane had to do with me and vice versa. My reverie was abruptly halted by Bowkett.

"Right bloke, get in." He practically pushed me into the plane behind the pilot then squeezed his bulk in beside me. There's not a lot of room in an Auster and with us and yet another 19 set behind the pilot there was even less. It was a tight squeeze. No sooner had we got in than the pilot took off which, to say the least, took me by surprise. I hadn't expected this.

"What's the trouble Sarge?", I asked.

"His signal is fading", said Bowkett.

The set was functioning O.K., nothing fundamentally wrong with it but as it only had a very short aerial and didn't have a High Power Unit I reckoned the range had to be limited and by now we were some miles away. No wonder it was fading. In fact we were over the German positions and they opened up with Ack-Ack but we got back safely

His third and final offering was in a walled orchard in the chateau grounds. It was full of slit trenches and blokes with radios, one of which needed attention. Whilst I am attending to the set someone in a nearby slit trench shouted for the Sergeant to take over while he went to the 'bog'. Bowkett went over, took the earphones off the signaller and stood by the side of the slit trench with the 38 set dangling from the headset and about a foot from the ground. Two things then happened in quick succession. Someone tried to contact the signaller whose set Bowkett had taken over and was frantically trying to get an answer, everyone was yelling at Bowkett to answer it but he seemed oblivious to it all! Then mortar bombs began to fall, dozens of them. Everybody shouted to Bowkett to get down. He just stood there apparently totally unconcerned and then suddenly dropped like a ton of bricks, not surprisingly. He'd been hit! I didn't see him again until we got back to Bulford.

At the quarry end of our field was a makeshift noticeboard on which we could read the progress of the war, a sort of daily bulletin. One day we got a shock. "A parade will be held at 0800 hours." Next morning, letting the war take care of itself, we dutifully assembled 'On Parade' in the field. In view hove a strange officer, well we hadn't seen him before; he must have come in on the boat. He was immaculately turned out, spick and span boots and brasses gleaming, Sam Brown belt and buckles bright. Sandhurst would have been proud of him, I'm not sure that we were. He then proceeded to give us a right old bollicking for being such a scruffy lot and I must admit he had a point. We washed and shaved and kept our weapons clean but the rest was, well - shit order. When you've lived in various holes in the ground, in the rain, being shot at and shelled and mortared, dug, humped, lifted and carried for about six weeks you tend to look slightly less than your best. I really think though that he came from another planet.

He finished his harangue by saying, "After all, this is no different to being on the Parade Ground at Bulford." Now I don't know if Jerry had been listening in or not but right on cue came the BRAFF, BRAFF, BRAFF of mortar bombs landing and before the next lot arrived our visitor from another world was alone and had learnt two things. Firstly, it was very MUCH different to the Parade Ground at Bulford and secondly, scruffy we may be but we could show him a clean pair of heels! There were no more parades and I don't remember seeing that extra-terrestrial any more.

We were still experiencing frequent shelling and one night it was particularly fierce. There were two of us that night with only one match between us so we chain smoked and Jerry shelled all night. The ground was heaving and I was slowly getting to the point where I wanted to jump out and go and shoot somebody, especially the bastards who were doing the shelling. Stupid of course, tantamount to suicide, but I learned that night what was meant by 'bomb happy', it's only one salvo away from 'shell shock'.

There were of course lighter moments. An ENSA show turned up and those 'off duty' could go. It was, where else, a couple of fields away. A stage had been assembled, microphone and loud speakers installed and we duly squatted in the field and waited. On came the two or three dancing girls to the tinkling piano and loud calls from the boys. Then came the comedian wearing an excessively tall top hat. He'd hardly got two words out when - you've guessed it - Jerry started to shell! Poor chap, he didn't know what to do with himself. Some wag then shouted, "Take your hat off they're shooting at your hat", and God help me - he did! That was the end of my one and only Ensa show, that was!

Another very welcome spell was a trip in a lorry to go to the cinema at Luc-Sur-Mer. This necessitated crossing the now famous Pegasus Bridge across the Orne Canal and the bridge over the Orne River. The latter bridge was still under observation by the Germans who still held high ground and although screens had been erected to hide the traffic the dust raised brought shells. A notice therefore had been erected which said, 'DRIVE SLOWLY, DUST BRINGS SHELLS'. Hardly anybody ever did, so the shells kept on coming. The film was Jennifer Jones in 'The Song of Bernadette' and I enjoyed it immensely and found it very moving particularly under the circumstances. It was a very strange feeling coming back to reality and war.

#11   The original Pegasus Bridge still in situ in 1984

Yet another fierce night bombardment had a strange outcome. Only one in about three shells were exploding. We could hear and feel them land so it was possible to estimate the frequency of explosions. After it was all over and I was beginning to fall asleep the Section Officer Lt. Gladwyn's deep voice was heard, "Hold, Hold"

"Yes Sir", I said.

"Did you hear those shells?"

"Yes Sir."

"How many would you say exploded?"

"About one in three Sir", I replied.

"Well keep a sharp look out in the morning they may be delayed action" and with that happy thought he departed.

The following day the truth proved to be most unusual. The shells had been filled with sand or some such non-explosive material and had obviously been sabotaged at source by Hitler's slave labour. How many lives they had saved by their actions God only knows.

Some time later I was taking Lt. Gladwyn to Luc-Sur-Mer and was held up at the "Dust brings shells" bridge while a lorry came across in the opposite direction. Just as the bridge was cleared a shell came screaming over our heads and buried itself in the ditch not two yards away and didn't explode!! My foot slipped off the clutch in fright and the jeep juddered. I got it under control and went over that bridge like a bat out of hell. A couple of miles down the road Rex Gladwyn said, "Pull over here and have a cigarette." My hands were trembling as I lit up and thanked God for brave slave labourers. I couldn't help wondering if Lt. Col. Smallman-Tew would forgive us. Sadly he was killed on 22 July at Escoville.

It was probably around this time that the Airborne Engineers built a corrugated iron and conduit pipe shower on a plateau on the escarpment and we were allowed, in properly organised groups, to take a shower. When you remember that we hadn't been able to have a shower or bath, in fact never had taken our clothes off, for about two months you can imagine what luxury we were about to enjoy. We duly stripped outside in the open, put our clothes in a tidy heap and romped into the shower about twenty at a time I would think. It was cold but it was heaven and we stood under the perforated conduit pipes and washed away the muck and sweat of two months. Then we got mortared. Everybody had but a single thought - to get out, get dressed and back down the slit trenches where it was comparatively safe. We ran out then stopped, realising we were now exposed in more ways than one and that we'd left the shelter of a corrugated roof and walls. We ran back in and roared our heads off at just how stupid we'd been. Habit however dies hard.

The weather was now glorious and it brought mosquitoes being so close to the canal. They got so bad one night I let them have my slit trench and slept in the open. The war seemed to be going pretty well and then we got a directive via the noticeboard to reinforce our slit trenches. "Oh! God," we thought, "not another attack." No, it wasn't. It was a 2000 bomber raid on Caen and the Yanks were involved – "Reinforce your slit trenches." We had a saying in those days "When the British shell, Jerry ducks, when Jerry shells the British duck. When the Yanks shell, everybody ducks." When I read and hear of all the hou-hah about so called 'Friendly Fire' in modern warfare and a handful of men being killed I can't help thinking it's a good job they weren't in the last lot. Mistakes are made by everybody and enquiries and post mortems are a waste of time and don't help the dead. Far better try to avoid doing it again instead of apportioning blame.

Those of us who could, stood on top of the escarpment and watched the bombers come in from the sea, fly over Caen, unload, turn and head back. The Yanks came in little tight groups, the RAF came in waves one above the other. The air was full of bombers. It was non stop and not a German plane in sight. Before long a huge column of black smoke rose from Caen and as I watched I wept. I still don't know why. Pity for the civilians, relief at Jerry getting his own back or the feeling that things were on the move? I just don't know but tears trickled down my face.

I always found time to write home every day even if it was only a page or two and wish the letters had been saved. I've forgotten so much that was probably contained therein. I also got mail from home regularly and particularly enjoyed the Giles cartoons Ena sent me. Betty Grable and Lana Turner also sent us sweets, or so we were told. We also got free issues of cigarettes from Montgomery with the message, "I'm sorry to have to keep you chaps for a little while longer, carry on the good work." After the third issue from Monty we were all in favour of telling him where to stick them and let us go home. Rumours were rife, somebody always knew somebody else who had it on good authority, or the Adj.'s batman was heard to tell so-and-so. If we believed half we heard we would be home every weekend that came along. "Have you heard the latest grif?", "What's the latest gen?". It became an epidemic.

As the pressure slackened life became more tolerable and a little more leisure time was possible. I learned to make lanyards from parachute cord and am glad to say I still have one. I also have a Pegasus made from the perspex of a Horsa glider cockpit. During one of those leisure moments I was sitting in glorious sunshine on the edge of "THE MAQUIS" writing home when two planes came over the top of the quarry. Looking up I saw the three white recognition bars on each wing and said, "It's O.K. they're ours." As I tumbled backwards down into the trench I thought, "If they were ours, why the hell did they open up?" I don't know if they were shooting at me but I took no chances.

Not long after that incident, a day or two at the most, our attention was caught by an unusual sound. Looking up we saw a V1 'doodle-bug', quite low really, 'Popping' its way towards the sea and England. There were a lot of uncomplimentary remarks about Hitler and the Germans from all the lads. Suddenly and inexplicably the doodle-bug did an about turn and 'Popped' its way back whence it came. The cheers that followed were deafening as we sent it on its way with shouts of, "See how you like that you bastards", etc., etc.

About the middle of August the Div. started to advance and fought its way through Pont L'Eveque, Pont Audemer, Trouville, Deauville and Honfleur to the Seine. The Battle of the Falaise Gap had been fought and won and we heard what was left of some of the Tiger tanks after the rocket firing Typhoons had finished with them. En route we stopped for a while near some German underground bunkers and went looking for souvenirs. Just outside one of the concealed entrances was a German helmet in pristine condition, brand new signs and all. It looked too good to be true and wary of booby traps I gingerly tied a rope to it, walked some distance away and pulled. Nothing happened except that someone else with a whoop of joy made off with my helmet. The bunkers were named after German Naval personnel Admiral Raeder, Hipper etc. and they were huge barracks capable of housing over a thousand I should think.

It was while en route to the Seine that on one stop we found a German telephone line snaking its way on the ground through a wood. The C.O. decided we should investigate, thinking it might lead to a bunker. We went through expecting at any moment to be fired on, but nothing happened and nothing was found. It was an anti-climax but I can't say I was sorry.

We met one of the real Maquis, i.e. Resistance movement, and I was invited to go with him to meet the rest. Why me I don't know, maybe because I could speak a little French! Whatever, I got permission from the C.O. and was taken on the pillion of a motor cycle to a nearby farm and met a bunch of French Resistance fighters. I chatted as best I could, shook hands all round, drank their cider and then I realised I had become the object of a heated conversation between them. I couldn't understand much of what was going on as they spoke so quickly and probably in patois. I did however gather that they were very interested in my rifle and I began to wonder if I would ever get back to the unit alive. I had the distinct feeling they would have loved to have the rifle for themselves. If so they must have thought better of it because after a while they all departed and I was taken back the way I came.

I think it was during this advance that at one stop near to an orchard some of the lads couldn't resist a spot of apple scrumping. The farmer, who must have been doing his own spot of guard duty, suddenly appeared on the scene. Beckoning us to follow him and saying "Bouvez, bouvez" he led us to a sunken barn-like structure housing two large barrels. For the next few minutes or so 'Entente Cordiale' was cemented as we toasted each other's countries in Normandy cider. The farmer had saved his apples and we had been saved a belly-ache. Which reminds me of a story I heard related many years afterwards at a reunion dinner.

One night near to the Div. HQ in Ranville, small arms firing broke out in an area where trouble was not expected. A small battle was going on. General Gale got hold of his Adjutant, Mike Hensman; who incidentally told the story; and told him to find out what the hell was going on and put a stop to it. It transpired that a group of Dutch soldiers had been eating cider apples and as a result had diarrhoea. They had gone into a wood to relieve themselves, moaning and groaning and jabbering away in Dutch, naturally, to each other. It so happened that the Paras were dug in and were holding that wood and on hearing the guttural language mistook it for German and consequently opened fire. The Dutch had returned their fire. As there were no casualties it made a very funny story but I don't think General Gale was amused.

I was in Deauville when the Div. started its journey home. Our task was now complete and there had been continuous fighting for three months. 821 had been killed, 2709 wounded and 927 missing. A total of 4457 casualties. With roughly 10,000 men in the Division the casualties were fairly high. Since the advance from Ranville on 17th August and in ten days of fighting, 400 square miles of enemy held territory were liberated and over 1000 German prisoners taken. Now we were going home and I can't tell you how glad I felt. I was very proud too, proud to have been there at the start of the greatest invasion in history.

Chapter 9   A Reputation to Uphold

We came home via the Mulberry Harbour at Arromanche and were ferried out to larger ships and had to climb aboard up the 'ladder' dangling over the side. It was a dicey business judging the rock and roll of both vessels, jumping and clinging like hell to the 'rope ladder' and then hauling yourself, fully kitted out, up to the top. Once there, many eager hands dragged you on board and wasn't I thankful for it. Assault courses after three months in Normandy I didn't want to know. I remember one poor lad losing his rifle off his shoulder as he struggled up the ladder. I expect it's still on the bottom of the sea off Arromanche. Once on board there was grub and hot sweet tea courtesy of the R.N. but most wonderful of all was newly baked white bread and butter. We hadn't seen bread for three months and we made pigs of ourselves. It was sheer heaven. We docked at Dover and made our way through a door at the base of the white cliffs, up a winding staircase inside the cliffs and came out in the courtyard of Dover Castle where we spent the night.

The next morning the Div. set off for home, Bulford. I however was nabbed by the C.O. Lt. Gladwyn and asked if I could find my way to Aldershot. In those days of course all road signs had been removed to confuse the enemy should he invade. Well the enemy hadn't invaded, quite the reverse, but the absence of road signs certainly confused me. Between us, however, we managed to reach Virginia Water which wasn't bad and not far from our destination. Stopping at Virginia Water we decided it was time to eat. Close by was a fenced-in, large hotel, standing in quite palatial grounds. We walked in through the gate and stood. There in front of us was a scene that to me looked like a Hollywood set. Obviously well-to-do people lounging by the pool side, in chairs beside tables, drinking in the sunshine and various alcoholic (I think) beverages. I just couldn't believe what I was seeing. In my naivety I thought all Britain was going through hard times and severely rationed. It was a rude awakening. What they thought of us with the mud of Normandy still visible God only knows. The C.O. said, "I think we'd better look somewhere else." We eventually found a cafe and had tea and scones. We also found Aldershot, spent the night there and continued on our way next day to Bulford.

We re-kitted and went home on a well earned leave from the 8th September to the 21st September. Fourteen glorious days in a brand new uniform. My leave coincided with the assault on Arnhem by the 1st A/B Div. and from the 17th - 25th September they took a hell of a pounding and the papers were full of their plight. Getting off the train at Newcastle station with my wife en route to friends in Gosforth I found myself being upbraided by a very irate woman for not being in Arnhem helping my comrades in their hour of need. I understood how she felt and sympathised with her but I also knew it was no good trying to explain that I'd just come back from Normandy and I was 6th A/B Div. not 1st - so I didn't. Ena however thought I should have.

Back from leave and we set to re-equipping. Jeeps and lorries came bare of all necessities and canvas awnings, hoods etc had to be fitted, Div. signs had to be painted. New charging engines to be tested, new sets, in fact everything was renewed and Sergeant Bowkett worked alongside and sweated as much as anyone - except Turner of course! This was the 'would be officer' who always managed to dodge duty.

It was after Normandy that he first made an appearance and I think he must have been one of our reinforcements. Turner just about drove Sergeant Bowkett mad. Whenever there was any work to do Turner could produce an 'Excused Duty' chit from the M.O. Yet on weekends he was always fit enough to get a weekend pass and buzz-off. It seems he had the system 'cracked'. He was also a tall, good-looking chap and was frequently seen in Salisbury wearing an officer-type trench coat, and carrying a stick and gloves. It was just outside Salisbury Station that I witnessed his finest performance.

On the night in question the last train to Bulford had gone but there was always the possibility of a lift in an Army truck - and so it proved. It was an R.A. lorry and we started to pile in the back and Turner, resplendent in his 'officer's gear', made a move towards the back of the lorry. Immediately from the passenger's seat in the cab jumped a Battery Sergeant Major, snapped up a salute and said to Turner, "Have my seat sir."

With a wave of his stick Turner said, "Thank you S.M.", climbed into the cab and was driven in style to Bulford. No one ever gave him away and apart from dodging work I think he was secretly admired. I often wonder what became of him. What a con man!

This was about the same time that our new uniforms were of a very high quality and we were allowed to wear collars and ties and put up a couple of medal ribbons. I must have looked very smart, so smart in fact that one evening, strolling down to the Garrison Theatre to check on performances, in the distance I saw an approaching soldier dump his fag fasten his collar and straighten himself up. As we passed he slung me a smashing salute. In reply I just smiled and said, "Evening." I could almost feel the knife in my back as I walked on.

Being Veterans of course made no difference to normal duty and guards and fatigues continued unabated. The RSM even decided to institute ceremonial 'Changing of the Guard' type duty and drilled us accordingly - we now had a reputation to uphold.

The first indication we had of the change in guard drill came whilst slow marching to the R.S.M.'s sweet serenade regarding the insanitary condition of his doorstep. He prowled up and down the line of stiff-backed and stiff-armed soldiers as we slow marched across the parade ground. Suddenly, pouncing like a hawk, he tapped me with his stick and barked, "You! Fall out over there." Me! What had I done? I duly complied, as did half a dozen other victims and we awaited our fate, which wasn't long in coming.

"Right", said R.S.M. Carr, "We now have a reputation to uphold so we are going to have a Ceremonial Guard and", pointing to us, "there they are." What had I done? Been too smart, that's what.

"This", he went on, "is your first Ceremonial Guard and I'm going to drill you myself until you are better than the Guards." Over the next few days he drilled and better drilled us until he was satisfied. Better than the Guards? I don't know but we were very smart and I was very proud to be on the first Ceremonial Guard Mounting, especially as we had an audience. It seemed like the entire camp turned out to watch.

Most duty officers were good enough to let it be known they were about to inspect the guard. At other times a telephone call to the guardroom from some 'informant' or runner would alert the duty Sergeant. Occasionally there was no warning and he suddenly appeared causing panic stations. That of course was fair and square, after all the guard is supposed to be always at the ready for anything. One night on one of these Ceremonial Guard duties it was my 'two hours on' and I spotted the duty officer approaching. Shouldering my rifle I marched rigidly along the veranda in front of the guard room and as I passed the open door shouted "Duty officer approaching" giving them time to put away the cards, put out the fags and put back the prisoners. With a 'Knee high' about turn I marched back to my position, halted, faced front, ordered arms and stood at ease. As the Duty Officer approached I came to attention and saluted him with 'present arms' which he acknowledged.

After he had inspected the guard including myself and he was leaving I repeated the performance. He hadn't been out of sight ten seconds when the guard commander came rushing out and said, "What the hell did you do?"

"I just presented arms Sarge", I said, wondering what I'd done wrong. "Why?"

"Because", he replied, "the Duty Officer came in and said to me, 'That's a very smart sentry you have out there Sergeant' - and it's the first compliment I've had as a guard commander - Well done." It also was the first compliment I had received but it wasn't the last. That came much later on in Palestine.

Morale was pretty high by now. Veterans all with new uniforms, collars and ties, medal ribbons, smart as a new pin and a reputation to uphold. We walked tall. Our Airborne and Pegasus flashes were now the silk and wool variety, all adding to the glamour.

One day someone came into the billet full of excitement. "Look what they've got in the tailor's shop" he said and showed us a simply superb flash. On a blue shield across the top of which was embroidered in gold on a black background 'ALLIED AIRBORNE'. In the centre was a silver 'No 1' with gold wings sprouting from its sides. Underneath that was a maroon cushion on which lay two silver daggers. It was one superb flash and we just couldn't wait to sew them on our sleeves. The camp tailor was delighted to see so many customers and sold his entire stock.

 # 12   The Allied Airborne flash worn (briefly) by members of 6th A/B Div. Sigs.

Next morning the 6th A/B Div. Sigs. stood on parade proudly wearing the new flash, awaiting the arrival of the R.S.M. Onto the parade ground strode R.S.M. Carr, took one look at us and had a screaming fit. "Get those effing things off! Who the hell told you to wear those effing things? Get those effing things off and be back on parade in five minutes!" We ran and he strode off with a face like thunder. Nobody had thought to inform us that they were American flashes, especially not the camp tailor. I still have it and treasure it and the memory.

By now it was generally felt that our next job would be somewhere in Germany and involve the Rhine. This feeling was strengthened when we embarked on a full-scale exercise. Div. Sigs. part in this as far as I was aware was to set up HQ somewhere on Salisbury Plain and get dug-in. This I proceeded to do assisted by Sergeant Bowkett, now recovered from his leg wound received in Normandy. I'd never had a Sergeant help me dig before but here he was, having chosen the site near to a clump of trees, digging away alongside me.

We got down about five feet and I thought that was deep enough but "No" said the Sarge. "Dig deeper bloke", so down we went another one and a half feet at least before he was satisfied. The fact that we couldn't see over the top didn't seem to matter to him nor the fact that only about six inches of the wireless aerial was protruding over the edge. Now I wasn't a wireless operator and as far as I knew neither was Sergeant Bowkett, although perhaps that was what he had originally trained as way back in his India days, so I had no idea what we were doing in a deep hole with a radio, but ours was not to reason why!

"You've gone a long way down Sergeant", came a voice and looking up, towering way above us stood General Gale!

"Yes Sir", said Bowkett as we slung up a hasty but precise salute. "Why is that Sergeant?", asked General Gale looking as genuinely puzzled as I was.

"Well Sir", said Bowkett, "Do you remember when we were in Normandy Sir?"

A long drawn out, "Yes I remember something about it", accompanied by a quizzical look from the General.

"Well Sir", said Bowkett, well into his stride and eager to show off his knowledge, skill and ability, "We got shelled a lot by the Germans because they'd D.F.'d us Sir,", (i.e. located our position by Direction Finding Equipment, which I'm sure was true), "and I'm making sure they won't do it next time."

I don't think it crossed Sergeant Bowkett's mind for one moment that if we'd stopped the Germans picking up our signals by burying the set and aerial we'd effectively stopped everyone else as well. In effect we'd rendered ourselves useless. It was a better own goal than the dinkle switch.

A guttural "Harrumph" came from the General and then another long drawn out, "Yes, I see! Carry on Sergeant", and acknowledging our salute he turned away and carried on with his inspection. I'm sure General Gale needed no further explanation and, discretion being the better part of valour, I thought it wise not to enlighten Sergeant Bowkett.

Not long after there were a number of changes in command at all levels in the Division and Major General E. L. Bols DSO replaced Major General Gale as Divisional commander on the 19th December 1944.

Chapter 10   Winter in the Ardennes

As things transpired we were involved in action again sooner than anticipated. Von Runsted broke through the American defences in the Ardennes on December 16th and in the early hours of the 22nd we were hauled out of bed and set off for the coast. On Christmas Eve we boarded ships and on Christmas morning landed in Ostend. What was galling was having seen all the Christmas fare, i.e. turkeys, Christmas pud, fruit, beer etc., being prepared for our Christmas dinner in Bulford and here I am with two sausages for breakfast in Ostend and no Christmas dinner to follow. What was even more galling, and I still resent it even today, was that on disembarkation I had a seat beside the driver of an LCV (Lorry Command Vehicle), an office, transmitting and receiving station with its own charging facilities and all necessary equipment. All very nice you may think and so it was. The galling bit came when Captain Hamer, now our Section Officer, Lt. Gladwyn having been made Adjutant, opened the door of the LCV and said, "Out! Take my bike, I'm in here."

Despatch riders are properly kitted out for their job, jerkin, riding breeches, boots, gauntlets and goggles. I had my army greatcoat, a scarf and a pair of woollen gloves. It was the worst winter in a hundred years with temperatures way below freezing. The roads were a sheet of glass, icicles two feet thick and snow piled high. The bike was a Matchless, I think, It was certainly a big one and heavy. I was to skid, slip and slide off it many times en route to the Ardennes and the further we traveled the colder and worse conditions got.

I suppose it was inevitable that on our way into the Ardennes we should meet a convoy of Americans on their way out. It was also inevitable that with thoughts of a totally ruined Christmas uppermost in their minds the A/B convoy should shower the Yanks with numerous ribald comments the most common of which was, "You're going the wrong effing way." The Yanks had been taken by surprise and overwhelmed by superior numbers and outflanked but they had fought hard so I don't suppose we could blame them. That however is with hindsight; at that moment it was good to get one over on the Yanks.

The road was very narrow and it was sometimes extremely difficult to pass each other and I well remember at one point, with a valley on the left and embankment on the right we came to a halt. On the right was a huge Yankee lorry - everything the Yanks had was bigger and better than ours of course although we'd had a sleepwalking Corporal who might have given them an argument on that score. Anyway, this lorry is on the right and on the left is a huge tree the roots and parts of which took up almost a third of the available space. An A/B jeep had come to a halt, unable to pass. The Yankee convoy was halted also and the lorry driver refused to or couldn't move an inch forward or back.

From somewhere behind me an A/B officer came forward to clear the way and stood in front of the jeep saying to the driver, "Come on, come on." Slowly he inched forward, his near side riding up the root and tree until the jeep was at an angle of 45^0. Everyone, except the officer apparently, could see it just wasn't possible and eventually the jeep driver left his vehicle and mad as a hatter stood nose to nose with this well-meaning but short-sighted officer and yelled, "What do you think I am driving, an effing matchbox?" The Yank convoy then started to move, the lorry vacated the area and the jeep was manhandled off the tree, onto the road and we resumed our journey. A cheerful little interlude in an otherwise grim day.

We eventually stopped in a little village sometime that evening, and we must have been travelling about 10 hours. I pulled up alongside the LCV and had to be practically lifted off the bike, I was frozen to the bone. Captain Hamer got out of the LCV with a look of great concern and a bottle of whisky in his warm hands and said "Have a drink." My hands were so frozen I couldn't hold the bottle properly and he had to help me. I took a drink, a sip really. "Have a good drink" he said, so cradling the bottle in my palms I tipped my head back and opened my throat and let it pour down. "Whoa, whoa! That's enough" he said and took the bottle and himself back to the warm LCV. Ten minutes later I could feel the life coming back into my limbs and I discovered my fingers and toes which I thought I'd lost 6 hours back. I've always remembered that whisky, I reckon it saved my life - Queen Anne was the name and I blessed her. I didn't bless Hamer but I was grateful for his whisky.

We were billeted that night in a small house in which were an old Belgian couple, I reckon 70-80 years old. By this time we had acquired sleeping bags which were very comfortable and the floor space was all we needed. It was noticeable that on the stove was simmering a pan of fairly clear liquid and a bare bone. Next morning the old couple made another meal from the same pan. They were obviously destitute so we went on the scrounge and gave them half a dozen tins of stew, bacon and fruit. We also gave the old man a tin of cigarettes. He then insisted on returning the compliment and pulling out a battered old tin rolled us each a cigarette from its contents. To please him we lit up, and coughed ourselves into tears. On enquiring what sort of tobacco it was he proudly showed us his tobacco crop from his back garden - unripened of course. He then volunteered the information that he added to that leaves from the trees. I left them with tears in my eyes not all due to Belgian 'tobacco a l'arbre'. They were my first civilians!

The cold was so intense that vehicles had to be started every quarter of an hour or so to stop them freezing and then it didn't always suffice. One of the jeeps started to boil and it was discovered that the hose connecting the radiator to the engine block had frozen. To the rescue came Sergeant Bowkett who grabbed the hose with one hand and started to bend it one way, then the other crunching the ice inside. "Keep the engine running bloke", said Sergeant Bowkett and bloke duly obliged. When an engine is running, so too is the fan and if you happen to put your thumb in its rotary movement you lose. Unfortunately for dear old Sergeant Bowkett he lost - the end of his thumb. Once again it was to be in Bulford that we next met.

My journey to the Ardennes ended in the grounds of the Chateau de Neffe, home of Prince Frederick de Merode, his wife Princess Elizabeth and their young son Prince Alexander and even younger daughter Therese. The Chateau was to become home to Div. HQ for the next six weeks and in that short space of time I was to form friendships which would be of great significance and last until today. Prince Frederick, I was to learn, was being held a political prisoner by the Germans. His wife, son and daughter had as a Chef and Mistress of the Household Monsieur and Madame Devillers, Camille and Emma. The children's governess was Nelly Simon. I dare say there were other servants in the house but it was with the former that I became acquainted and finally life-long friends. It all began when I was coming back from the cookhouse with my meal frozen solid in my mess tin.

The grounds of the Chateau were immense, acres of woodland in which deer hunts were held. The deer were roe-buck, chevreuil in French which was the language in that part of the Ardennes - but why not, the Princess was connected to the French Royal Family. There was also a lake at the bottom of a valley on the other side of which was the old chateau now used as a farm. The old chateau was the cookhouse and by the time I'd walked back to my appointed station near the new Chateau with my meal it was frozen solid. It would be very early on when a chap said to me, "What is that?", and when I'd told him it was my dinner he said it was frozen and I couldn't eat it. I said I would heat it first and he said, "Come with me." All this of course was in my best schoolboy French but it sufficed and he was obviously pleased we could converse, however haltingly. It was Camille the chef and he took me into the kitchen, introduced me to his wife, Emma, put my dinner in the oven and produced a bottle of Belgian beer.

The kitchen, below stairs of course, was huge, as was the oven, and in the middle was a huge wooden table. It put me in mind of a medieval castle kitchen. That was the start of a wonderful friendship which lasted until the day when sadly he died. That happily was many years in the future. From that moment on I ate regularly 'below stairs' with Camille and Emma, shared their beer and they shared my cigarettes. Eventually I was invited to their quarters which were right at the top of the Chateau. I climbed those stairs many times, had wonderful fractured French/English conversations with them and established a truly wonderful rapport.

 # 13   The Chateau de Neffe in 1954

The LCV, the main HQRA communication link, was my responsibility, maintenance wise, and I was never far away. By now we had graduated from sleeping in holes in the snow in our sleeping bags to a barn like structure which gave us shelter from the below zero conditions in which we not only had to survive but work. I was in the LCV on New Years Eve 1944 -1945 when the rum ration came round. Three or four of the lads being non rum drinkers donated their ration to me and I ended up with an enamel mug almost full of rum. I managed to climb to the top of the Chateau de Neffe without spilling a drop and saw the New Year in with Camille and Emma. With my rum and cigarettes and Camille and Emma's beer and haute cuisine goodies we had one hell of a night. I was privileged and I knew it but I also respected it and them. Without exceeding the bounds of propriety, and as duty permitted, I became part of the family and Camille and Emma, Nelly Simon and I became very good friends.

 # 14   Camille and Emma Devillers

One of the biggest laughs we ever had was when Camille and I got into a political discussion one night and he finished by saying that no matter if it was the Democrats, Communists or Fascists who were in power he would still have to work for a living. I then tried to tell him that he was a philosopher. Not knowing the French equivalent of philosopher I tried to make the English word sound French and said "Vous etes un fil-osof-fur."

His reaction was to open his mouth and eyes wide and say, "Quoi?" So I repeated my statement. "Moi?", he said, "moi, un fil-osof-fur?, and I said, "Oui", wondering what was wrong. He roared his head off and took a laughingly long time to explain that I'd just called him a bicycle. It was my turn to have a good laugh. I think it must have been our equivalent of a velocipede. It was one helluva laugh and we enjoyed it for days afterwards.

Years later at a Pilgrimage in Ranville I was to meet George Frith who had a similar story from Neffe. It seems that he and a pal were having a problem digging-in without the aid of a shovel so he went to the farm and in his best French asked the farmer "Avez-vous un" - and not knowing the French for shovel made it sound French - "avez-vous un shov-ell?"

"Cheval monsieur?", queried the farmer.

"Oui", said George. Off went the farmer and returned with a horse! What else?

All the time I was at Neffe the Paras and Air Landing Brigade were involved in the fighting around Bure and the artillery were also in action. Compared with Normandy however I was having an easy time, my worst enemy being the bitterly freezing weather and working conditions it engendered. In time we were no longer needed in the Ardennes and after six weeks we took our leave. I said my goodbyes, promised to keep in touch, which I subsequently did, and set off on my motor bike down the drive and, just before I disappeared from view, I turned in the saddle to wave goodbye and promptly fell off. There's nothing to beat leaving them with a laugh!

Chapter 11   Hospitality in Holland

We moved to Holland to an area between Venlo and Roermond on the banks of the Maas. Div. Sigs. HQRA went to Panningen and we spent the first night in a big house which I learned years later belonged to a doctor. It had a large staircase at the top of which, in the ceiling, on the landing was a stained glass 'light'. Above that was the attic the entrance to which was up some more stairs and through a trap door situated to the left of the 'light'. We were billeted in the attic. In the centre was the brick chimney running up through the roof and at the base of the chimney breast was a small recess minus fire grate. It was bitterly cold and some enterprising bloke lit a fire in the recess and we settled down for the night.

In the small hours of the morning we woke up coughing in an attic full of smoke and a dull red glow emanating from the chimney breast. It wasn't a fireplace so much as an air vent and the timbers in the chimney breast were glowing. Quick as a flash, if you'll pardon the pun, we were standing around the glowing timbers peeing with all our might. To the smoke and coughing was now added steam and stench but for Airborne Initiative it wasn't a bad effort. By now we could hardly breathe, someone said "Let's get out of here" and there was a bit of a rush for the trap-door during which George Atkinson, just in front of me, stepped onto that beautiful stained glass light. I managed to grab him before he went crashing to the floor below and it took a couple of us to haul him back.

We were moved, or should that be evicted, and spread around Panningen and I with about six others found ourselves billeted at Schoolstraat 16, our hosts being the Heuvelmann family. The family consisted of the mother, two sons and three daughters, the father was in a labour camp and Aunt Maria a schoolteacher lived on the other side of the street. Willy was the eldest son and had, during the occupation, feigned madness to avoid being conscripted into forced labour. To that end he had sought refuge and been cared for by the brothers in the nearby Monastery. Luke was the youngest son and a little rip. Mia, Truus and Bernadette in descending order were the delightful daughters and with the exception of Willy they were all school children. The family vacated their bedrooms and they slept in the cellar.

I set up my charging engine in the back yard/garden where I also kept my bike which had now become a two-stroke. I remember it well because one day young Luke pinched it and roared off into Panningen. I nearly had kittens. He was just a boy and at risk and God knows what repercussions an accident would have started. I was more concerned however about him. Thankfully all went well but he got a good telling off when he returned. I soon made friends with the children and used to sing to them and draw pictures for them, mostly cartoons of Mickey Mouse, Donald Duck, Pluto and Popeye.

The weather continued to be bitterly cold and the constant traffic made slush of the snow which wasn't at all pleasant. We had a cookhouse of sorts situated in the village and I remember one very sad sight. A young Dutch girl scantily clad with a very young baby begging food. Apparently she had nowhere to go because the baby had been fathered by a German soldier. She was an outcast. I was to see also one or two girls with shaven heads being shunned for having consorted with the enemy. Needless to say we fed them all. Apparently, if I could believe what I heard, there were those who didn't object to consorting with British soldiers. One morning in the queue for breakfast I could hear one of the blokes who was dishing food out describing in graphic detail his handling of a girl the previous night. When I got to the counter he handed me a slice of Dutch cheese on which I could see his filthy fingerprints - hungry as I was I declined.

 # 15   Schoolstraat Panningen

Willy and I got on very well as he could speak a good bit of English. I also learned the odd word or two in Dutch and even managed to make myself understood to Mother Heuvelmann who was a lovely, quiet soul. What a burden she had to bear during those occupation years only she knew. Small wonder the Dutch were glad to see us. The Germans had looted the land taking all the food and in particular the menfolk. I believe the Allies saved a lot of lives by dropping food to the Dutch. During those six weeks, as in Neffe, I became one of the family. Willy taught me the Latin words of 'Ave Maria' and 'Panis Angelicus' and he also taught me a war time song which began 'Warrom Wou Jy' and wrote the words on a little card which I carried with me right through the war. I was surprised one day to receive, through Willy, an invitation from Father Pypers, rector of the Monastery, to go and sing to the Brothers. I was happy to do so and thoroughly enjoyed myself and so I think did they.

Life in Panningen was quiet. The Germans 8th Para Division were on the other side of the Maas and the front line troops were largely occupied with patrol work across the river into enemy-held territory. Constant probing, observing and taking the odd prisoner. A daily bulletin was posted to keep everyone in the picture and whatever else may have been happening everyone began to take a special interest in 'Hans'. 'Hans' was the name given to a particular German soldier who was observed daily coming down to the river bank to relieve himself in a clump of bushes. He became quite a celebrity on our side of the Maas and his daily defecationary activities were eagerly awaited and religiously reported. Sadly, one day we read that there would be no further bulletins on 'Hans' as some spoilsport had shot him! Maybe 'Hans' had enjoyed showing his backside to the British, I don't know, but someone had obviously got sick of looking at it. I couldn't help wondering if he'd been shot before, after or during!

Wanting to somehow say thank you to the family for their kindness the chance occurred when a film show was organised and I invited Willy to join me. I was initially surprised at the reaction but I came to appreciate it and understand. The Heuvelmanns were a devout and staunch Catholic family and when Willy asked permission from his Mother to go to the Cinema it had to be established that it was a wholesome and proper film for Willy to see and would in no way expose him to 'the flesh and the devil' I think is the best way to put it. As the film was Bing Crosby in 'Going My Way' I had no hesitation and no problem in putting their minds at rest. Willy's susceptibilities were in no way tarnished and he enjoyed the film. In later years he was to be ordained as a Catholic priest and in due time rose to the exalted position of Dean of Roermond. I often wonder if, after Confessional, he ever looked back to those innocent years.

About this time Div. HQ needed D.C. bulbs rather urgently. I was detailed to go to Eindhoven with George Atkinson, find the Philips factory and bring back as many D.C. lightbulbs as we could get. I duly drove George to Eindhoven and cruised about looking for the Philips factory. Eventually George said, "We'll stop and ask this fella."

"Excuse me", said George slowly, and in his best Yorkshire accent, "Excuse me, but can you tell me where Philips factory is. You know, Philips factory, for lightbulbs. Electric lights." And while he was speaking George was drawing, in the air, with his finger, a picture of a building, a light bulb and switching it on and off with his other hand. After a few minutes of this pantomime trying desperately to make the Dutchman understand him he paused for breath.

The Dutchman who had watched his performance with interest then said "Yes, Philips factory is just ...", etc., etc., and directed George to his goal in perfect English!

The look on George's face was one of amazement as he said, "Thanks, thank-you", and climbed back into the jeep. "I didn't know he could speak English", said George. "Why didn't he say something?"

"I think he was enjoying the pantomime too much to spoil it", I said.

When we got to the factory we explained our needs, without the pantomime, and there was much discussion amongst the staff. It transpired that they had no D.C. bulbs in the factory but after much searching of records said they knew where to find them. Accordingly some of the staff boarded the jeep and took us out into the countryside, after driving a few miles we were directed into a farmyard. Much discussion between the farmer and the Philips officials resulted in us being led into a barn. Then it was bales of hay to move and there at the back of the barn, under the hay, were boxes of light bulbs. Thankfully we took what was offered, took the officials back to Eindhoven and the bulbs back to Panningen. I was intrigued, we'd just had a demonstration of the lengths the Dutch would go to, to avoid helping the Germans. Apparently Philips had hidden their stock all over Holland. I was glad I'd seen it.

Towards the end of February we took our leave but the day before departure we had a whip-round and bought about six tins of apricots at the NAFFI, it was all they had on offer, and gave them to Mother Heuvelmanns! I said my goodbyes and promised to keep in touch, which I did.

We came back to England and docked at Tilbury and were given shore leave. Some of us got off the ship in double quick time thereby missing the order cancelling shore leave. On returning to the LST around 11 p.m. there it wasn't! Panic stations! After frantic enquiries from other vessels we found it was on the other side of the Thames. How to reach it? No problem, There was a ferry further up river. It was further up river than I thought and by the time I reached it on foot the last ferry had sailed!! Double panic! "Never mind", said the Navy lads, "there'll be another in the morning, in the meantime you can bunk with us." With thoughts of, "You're on a charge", "You'll be Court-martialed", "You'll get shot", "You're a deserter", I settled in a bunk on a landing craft and spent a fitful night.

Came the dawn and after a smashing breakfast of bacon, sausage, beans and eggs I caught the first ferry across the Thames only to find a deserted quayside!!! After walking around looking for signs of life I eventually found an RTO hut and a bunch of lost souls in the same predicament as myself. The Transport officer was having a great time and found us a lorry into which we all piled and set off in hot pursuit of 6th A/B Div. convoy which had left for Bulford during the night. It was some time before we caught up with them, joined on the tail end and eventually ended up back in Bulford. Apart from having the urine well and truly extracted there were, thankfully, no further repercussions. I went home on leave 1st - 8th March. On my return it was business as usual re-equipping and out on exercise.

It was about now that I was sent with a team to join the American 17th A/B Div. at Upper, Nether or Middle Wallop, or was it Lower? The purpose of the visit was to net our sets to their frequencies and it took us about a week. During this time we billeted in a 'Spider', so called because it consisted of 8 huts terminating at a central point, as in a spider's web, the central point being the ablutions and recreational area etc. We drew our own rations from the Yankee stores which we then passed on to them for cooking. It was an eye-opener. How many eggs did we want? Three dozen? Can't be bothered with piddling numbers - take a case! Bacon? 2lb? Take a side followed by a huge joint of beef, a sack of potatoes, onions etc. etc. etc. Those Yanks didn't do things by half. We were also introduced to Yankee K rations which was their equivalent of our 24 hour ration pack except theirs was superior - naturally - well at least it had a lot of candy bars in it.

I remember at least one very funny incident in the cookhouse whilst queuing for a meal. The Yanks didn't use plates or mess tins, instead they had a large tray in which had been pressed out various sized and shaped indentations to take the various offerings from the cooks. As you walked along the counter you received a dollop of potato, after which you presented another part of the tray to receive the next offering etc. One of our lads deep in conversation with the chap behind him walked slowly along this long counter and received in the middle of his tray, potato. On top of that he got veg, meat, gravy, corn on the cob, prunes and custard all in one glorious heap. It created quite a lot of fun, especially with the Yanks. After that little diversion it was back to Bulford.

Chapter 12   The Rhine Drop

On the 19-20 March we moved into a transit camp somewhere close to an airfield which I was to know as 'Mushroom Farm'. Briefing was short, sharp and a shock! Into a wooden hut I went with a bunch of others and, on a detailed model, discovered my glider, one of six landing in the same field, was to land right at the front door of a farm (a German strong point - weren't they all?) bristling with troops and machine guns. It was situated somewhere in the Diersfordt wood area on the other side of the Rhine and not far from Hamminkeln. I came out of the briefing and looked in the direction of where I thought Sunderland might be and said, "I'm sorry but I won't be coming home this time." Defeatism? I don't think so. I felt it was a fair assessment of my chances. I'd been there before and knew what was coming or thought I did. I really didn't think I was going to survive. I thank God and the Yanks that I did.

I can only recall two of my co-passengers as we took off from Mushroom Farm in the early hours of 24th March and set off for the Rhine. They were two American Sergeants, both wireless ops, one of whom was nicknamed 'Muscles' and the other a silver-haired chap who I called 'Tom Mix' after the silent movie cowboy, because he looked just like him. There was a jeep and trailer in which was housed their radio transceiver and I apparently was there to see that it functioned O.K. I remember very little of the flight except that somewhere over Belgium the British 6th and American 17th A/B Divs. converged and flew on towards the Rhine. Many years afterwards I learned that they met up somewhere above the fields of Waterloo which I still think was a beautifully poetic touch.

How I came to be in a glider with an American team or vice versa I never did find out and can only assume they were a radio link between the British 6th and American 17th A/B Div. at HQRA level. It was around 11 a.m. on a beautiful sunny Saturday, 24 March 1945, when we landed right on target, well at least we were at a farm and one hell of a battle was going on. The noise was terrific and when the glider came to a halt we momentarily went flat and froze.

If it had been an American movie I would have expected John Wayne to suddenly appear and take command instead of which I heard myself shouting, "We can't stop here all day, let's get this glider unloaded and get the hell out of here." The Horsas had been modified since the difficulties experienced with the tail sections on D-Day. The cockpit and nose section had now been hinged and as mine swung open I was able to jump out into battle 'Straight from the Horsa's mouth'.

A stationary glider is a sitting duck and the proof, if needed, was in front of me. On the other side of the field lay a Horsa, smoke pouring from its fuselage and as I looked a figure came staggering out and stood lost, bewildered, bomb-happy. I dashed over and said "Hang on, I'll get the others out" and he said, "They're all dead." He obviously had a head wound as his face was covered in blood and as a result he was half blinded. Slinging his arm round my neck I half carried him into the farmyard and sat him down behind a dung heap, at least it was

 # 16   British and American gliders near Hamminkeln 25/03/1945

Photograph courtesy of the Imperial War Museum, London (B5428)
The distinctive shapes of two Horsas can be seen towards the bottom left of the picture.
The cockpit of the nearest has been swung open for unloading.

better shelter than an open field. Telling him to stay there I went looking for a medic. I couldn't find one so went back to see how he was and he'd gone!

I then went back to my glider to help with the unloading, which was a lot easier than in Normandy. No sooner were we out and ready to move off when a yell came from 'Muscles',

"Teddy Boy, Teddy Boy, the set's not working, we're off the air."

"Oh! My God", I thought, "Apart from fundamentals what do I know about Yankee radios?" A quick check proved the power was disconnected and a quick look found the battery lead which had been 'kicked off' during the unloading. In just a few moments radio communication was re-established and the Yanks duly impressed.

"Gee" said 'Muscles' "that was a great job, you'd have got a medal for that in our outfit." I'm inclined to think he meant it.

By now the 'local' gunfire had subsided and we moved away from the farm leaving the dead and wounded behind. 'Tom Mix' and 'Muscles' went their own merry way as there was no room for me in a heavily laden jeep and trailer and I never saw them anymore. I joined up with a bunch of blokes who were following a leader who apparently knew where we were going. I was glad of that because I didn't even know where I'd been - and I still don't! Somewhere in the Diersfordt Wald and somewhere close to the DZ of the American 17th A/B Div. for sure, and two things make me absolutely certain.

First, as we made our way through the fields after we left the farm I saw dozens of dead Yankee parachutists, some still hanging from trees and some hanging over fences. There hadn't yet been time to recover them. It was at that precise moment that my appreciation of Yanks changed dramatically. I now knew that whatever else I had thought they were real soldiers and could fight and die alongside the rest and in all probability having landed just ahead of me I owed my life to them.

The second thing is that we followed and eventually crossed a railroad track and in doing so left it at a small railway station on the platform of which were scattered railway tickets. I picked a few up as souvenirs. I still have four of them and they read:- Diersfordt - Emmerich, Diersfordt - Wesel, Diersfordt - Diusberg Merderich Sud and Diersfordt - Drevenack. I think it is enough confirmation that I had just left Diersfordt Railway Station. I'm inclined to think I landed on or very close to the American, rather than the British, DZ.

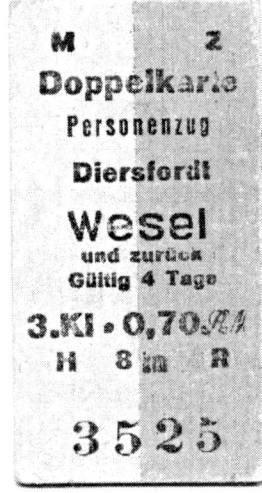   

17   Rail tickets picked up at Diersfordt station on 24/03/1945

However! Passing through the railway station and up an incline through the fields we came to a halt at a roadside which had a commanding view of the countryside we had just left. I was now among members of my own Div. and a wedge had been dug out of the ground into which had been parked a trailer containing a radio link. We were now employed filling sandbags with earth to protect said radio link. Some are digging, others filling and the rest building a sandbag wall. I am on my knees, filling. One of the lads who was digging stopped for a moment and said, "God, my leg's not half stiff." His leg was inches from my nose and when I looked I could see a V shaped tear in his trouser leg!

I immediately said, "You've been hit."

"Don't talk so effing stupid", came the reply. After one or two pleasantries in the same vein I persuaded him to drop his trousers and there exposed to his view was a swollen, purple and angry red hole in his leg. He took one look and promptly fainted. God knows how long he'd had a bit of shrapnel in his leg, probably from landing. He was carted off and we finished the sandbagging.

Then someone, an officer I think, decided we should eat and would anyone rustle up a meal and what made me volunteer God only knows but I did. There was one stipulation said the officer, It must be a hot meal. Milk and eggs in the farmlands was no problem, where the flour came from I don't know, probably the same farm. I made a batter, opened up some bully and fried up corned beef fritters. It was our first meal since leaving England and it went down very well - with tea of course.

It was getting late by now and it was decided to bed down for the night. All opposition in the area had been overcome and it was safe enough for the night. Where to rest? On the corner was a barn, an ideal spot I thought and made for it with my sleeping bag. Standing on the roadway beside the barn was a bunch of Yanks who said, "I wouldn't go in there, bud, if I was you." On enquiring why I was informed that the barn was full of German grenades.

"Well, shift them", I said!

"Like hell", came the reply, "we're not going in there." In I went and found it was just as they'd said, full of German grenades - the 'stick' or 'potato masher' type. It was also full of straw, just fine to sleep on.

Backwards and forwards I went carrying four grenades on each trip and laid them in a neat row in the ditch on the opposite side of the road. I was watched the whole time by those same Yanks - from a safe distance. When I was finished I grinned at them and said, "It's safe now, you can go in."

"Gee, bud", said one of them, "That was a hell of a brave thing to do, you'd have got a medal for that in our outfit."

I thought, "I'm doing well, two Yankee medals in one afternoon", and, thus decorated, bedded down for the night in the straw in the barn. Next morning I awoke with a pain in the back and thought I must have been sleeping on a turnip, but not so, I had missed one grenade.

Moving out from that barn I found myself sitting on top of a heavily laden trailer and as we moved off a figure appeared in a ditch, aiming, so I thought, a gun at us and I reached for my Sten only to realise next minute that it was an American photographer, so somewhere I'm on film but I doubt if I'll ever see it. It's probably just as well if I looked as I felt - foolish.

Chapter 13   Advance to the Baltic

After so many years it is impossible to remember everything in chronological order and in any case the advance of the 6th A/B Div. from the Rhine to the Baltic only took six weeks and I believe at that time was the fastest advance in modern war history. At one stage I believe we were even out of radio communication with the troops in the rear but that is by the way. In the early days we were moving through the farmland and small villages and as each overnight stop, whenever we did stop, was at a farm we soon learned to forage for eggs and chickens and bottled fruits and hams and sausages from the cellars. I suppose it could be called looting but to us it was the spoils of war and a welcome addition to Army rations.

\# 18   Brewing up in Germany on the way to the Baltic in April 1945

Travelling through the farmlands of Germany in convoy you automatically followed the vehicle ahead without knowing where or when you were going to stop. As the Div. was making a beeline for the Baltic we tended to stop only when opposition was met or we were camping for the night.

On one occasion, late in the afternoon, I had to stop and change a punctured wheel on the trailer I was towing. By the time we'd unloaded the trailer, naturally the wheel being the last thing out, the convoy had disappeared from sight. It was then we discovered that the wheel was the wrong size. Only one thing to do, unhitch and repack the trailer and put it on the roadside and chase after the convoy. Off we roared and after a mile or so we caught up with the convoy, unpacked a lorry to find a spare wheel - and weren't they happy - and set off back to the trailer leaving the convoy to get still further ahead. Having changed the wheel, once again we set out to find the convoy. By now it was dusk and not another soul was in sight and there we were driving through Germany, two lonely blokes in a jeep and trailer and fully expecting to be fired on from left, right or centre at any minute. It was an eerie sensation to say the least but on we went, full of apprehension, through the deserted farms with the odd dead horse and cow in the fields on either side and one particularly sad and sickening sight - a dead 'frau' in the roadside.

Just after that came the most spine-tingling and ear-splitting shrieks which set our hair on end, stopped us dead in our tracks and set hands to weapons. We couldn't tell what the hell was happening until the shrieks and squeals got closer and out of the gloom a tiny piglet came racing down the road doing its nut. Having foraged our way from the Rhine the first thought was "bacon" and, war forgotten, we chased that pig all over until we eventually caught it, found a sack and, despite its kicking and squealing, stuffed it in.

Standing it in the well of the jeep off we set. It was dark now so it was with great relief that we found the convoy encamped for the night in yet another farm and slinging the sack over my shoulder I set off to find the rest of the lads. Passing a group of officers who were examining a map the pig decided it was time for another squealing session and duly obliged much to their surprise.

"What have you got there?", said one of them, to which I replied

"A pig, sir"

"Let me see it", he said and I did. "What are you going to do with that?", he asked.

"Bacon, sir" said I, highly delighted. The delight was short lived.

"It's far too small", he said, "Let it go!"

"But", I said.

"And that's an order!", he barked.

"Sah", said I and sadly went to find the rest of the Section.

By a strange coincidence we were spending the night in a long shed one side of which was a pigsty housing about a dozen or so fairly large pigs. I dumped my piglet among them and all hell broke loose as they converged on the tiny intruder and chased it in and out of the various compartments of the shed-length pen. Backwards and forwards they went and the noise was deafening. It was 'Yoicks - Tally Ho' and the lads cheering them on. Suddenly the older pigs stopped the chase, put their heads together, had a grunting conference, and then took up the chase again. This happened twice. Eventually peace reigned and we slept, they in their half of the sty and we in ours, albeit in sleeping bags.

Next morning we set off, my jeep loaded with hams, bottled fruits, eggs, the odd chicken, and German sausages - but no bacon! Not far down the road I suddenly burst out laughing and couldn't stop. My passenger, looking around for the reason for the hilarity and finding none, said, "What the hell are you laughing at?" Between fits of laughter I tried to explain that I'd just had a vivid vision of a puzzled, bewildered and mystified German farmer's face as he looked at his latest 'arrival' - And THIS little piggy came from NOWHERE!!!

By now the 'Sea and land' contingent of the Div. had caught up with us and Derek Hogarth was once again amazed to find any of us alive but at the same time, of course, very pleased to see us all again. I think it was shortly after this that our advance Div. HQRA was held up by a group of Germans in a wood on the left-hand side of a crossroads. It must have been a group the Paras had missed or had by-passed or who had lain 'doggo' for a while, but here we were being stopped by their fire. What followed was a delight to see. A dozen or so jeeps, heavily armed with Bren guns, raced alongside the wood and opened up a prolonged and concerted fire which made the timbers fly and in no time at all the Germans surrendered and were sent back to the rear - and the advance continued.

Sometimes, depending on the circumstances encountered, it was necessary to travel at night and I well remember two such occasions. Night convoys were very difficult due to lack of vision. Lights were taboo for obvious reasons and in the open country and on moonless nights it was pitch black. We did however have tiny lights fitted underneath vehicles which shone a very small torch-like beam onto white-painted back axles, which gave some help to following vehicles.

On the occasion I recall however this wasn't sufficient for some idiot who momentarily switched his headlights on to get a better look at the situation. This of course temporarily blinded those behind who resorted, temporarily of course, to similar tactics. The result was a dot, dash, dot, dash Morse Code of lights along the convoy and brought a lot of angry yells of, "Put those effing lights out!" from those with more sense. It also brought a great big "Danke" from the crews of the Tiger tanks strategically sited and tucked away on the edge of a wood three of four hundred yards away who, having almost 180 degrees of road and therefore convoy within view, proceeded to pound us with everything they had. They did quite a lot of damage before they were driven off.

On another occasion the convoy pulled off the main road into open fields at dead of night and it was again pitch black. Digging slit trenches was impractical so, having sleeping bags, we got into a fairly deep ditch alongside a hedge and crawled on hands and knees feeling for somewhere level enough to bed down for the night. Derek Hogarth, who was ahead of me, suddenly leapt screaming out of the ditch and ran, still screaming and waving his arms about like a madman, into a dimly lit bell-tent full of officers who were in deep discussion re the plan of battle which they had marked out with coloured pencils on their talc-covered maps. Derek was hotly pursued by a swarm of extremely angry hornets into whose nest he had just seconds previously stuck his hand. For a few seconds more there was a silhouetted war dance visible on the tent wall before the occupants exploded into the night still hotly pursued by the same hornets intent on wreaking revenge for the destruction of their home. Chaos and curses ensued for some time afterwards but from the zipped-up depth of my sleeping bag I could now only hear it. Peace eventually reigned and I went out like a light, totally exhausted.

Came the dawn and I am surrounded by artillery shell cases from the guns on the other side of the hedge. I still can't believe it. They must have been pounding away all night and I hadn't heard a thing. Or had those shell cases been there earlier? I think not or I would have felt them as we crawled along the ditch.

The big question now was where was Hogarth? Even some of the officers joined in the hunt, intent I think on murdering him, but at last we found him. Actually, we heard him first, moaning and whimpering in the bottom of a trailer and covered by a tarpaulin. He had every right to moan being in so much pain and what a sorry sight he was, face and head all swollen with stings. They'd even got in his mouth, down his neck and up his arms and legs, and of course his hands. The poor lad was delivered into the tender care of the medics and it was some time before he was fit for anything. Some of the officers had copped it too but not as badly as poor Derek. The hornets had even managed to get between the talc covers of the maps and now, added to the blue, green and red arrows and circles of the battle plan, was the black and yellow of squashed hornets!

Encamped in a clearing in a forest one day we had a breakdown in radio communications which wasn't surprising as we were surrounded by trees 60-100 feet in height.

Added to which was the limited range of our transmitters. From somewhere and somehow an Australian Signals Officer appeared on the scene - well he sounded and looked like one, bush hat and all - and told us to sling an aerial up in the trees. The aerial he offered was uninsulated copper wire. I couldn't help feeling he might as well stick it straight in the ground and thought about Sergeant Bowkett. He, poor chap, had been killed on landing, charging a machine gun post with his Sten gun. Forty years later I was to visit his grave in the Reichwald Forest and learn he was an only son and his name was Tom. I missed him!

We were halted on a roadside which ran parallel to a river which flowed along the bottom of a very steep valley. The road eventually turned right and continued down a very steep hill, across a bridge and up the side of another very steep hill. The river I think was the Weser of Pied Piper fame. MPs stood at the top of the bank and allowed one vehicle at a time to go hell for leather down the bank, across the bridge and up the other side. The reason being that a Stuka dive bomber was stooging around and now and then diving almost vertically down to bomb or strafe the bridge. The blokes who hadn't yet got near to the 'off' congregated on the top of the bank to watch the 'fun' and I was one such when someone behind got so mad or frustrated that he opened up on this Stuka with his Bren. Almost at the last second realisation dawned that he was following the Stuka as it dived on the bridge and our heads would be in the line of fire. With various cries of "You effing idiot" "You stupid bastard" and other unprintable epithets we went flat and thankfully kept our heads on our shoulders. The MPs weren't all that pleased either. Oh! By the time we got over, the bridge was still intact.

One day I was grabbed by Captain Hamer - shades of Sergeant Bowkett - and given the job of equipping, from scratch, a brand new LCV. It was a rush job as it was to replace the old LCV which some idiot had set alight whilst filling the charging engine, which was still running, and totally destroyed the LCV and all it contained, especially the radio. HQRA was off the air. It was an impossible task for one man, and he knew it, so a team of us set to work and drilled holes for aerials and cables through the roof and from compartment to compartment. We fitted aerial mountings and aerials, installed office equipment and telephones, a brand new Canadian transceiver and batteries and associated connectors and cables, a new charging engine and intercom system, office to radio operator to driver.

Captain Hamer worked with us right through the night, non-stop and in 36 hours we were back on the air. It was one hell of a job but we got no medals. The sequel was very funny. A few of the lads had their gear, kit bags etc on the LCV and of course that all went up in smoke too. Captain Hamer said that anyone who had lost kit in the fire could indent for new and it was unbelievable how much kit had been carried on that LCV!!! Everybody in the Section indented for new gear. Well, it was too good a chance to miss wasn't it?

It was becoming noticeable as we bashed on to the Baltic that the number of German prisoners was increasing. They walked past us in scores then hundreds, many seemingly without escort, certainly without weapons and most certainly without transport. Any German vehicles going back down the lines to captivity were confiscated by the Div. and the occupants, irrespective of rank, were made to walk. I think it would be pretty true to say that before we reached the Baltic there were in our convoy as many German vehicles as British. We even took their bicycles from them. "Walk, you bastard, walk" was the order of the day! The scent of victory was in our nostrils even though we still had a long way to go and we began to feel invincible.

We left the open countryside and farms behind eventually and encountered more and more villages but before that happened I suffered one very nasty experience. It happened in the open bare earth 'farmyard' of a building which I think, besides being a farm, was also a corn and hay merchants. I suddenly got the most violent pain in the gut and I thought I'd been wounded. The pain was intense and had me holding my belly and rolling around on the ground, knees under my chin and my face contorted with agony. I wept and cried out in pain to no avail. I thrashed around to no avail, the agony persisted. How long this went on I don't know; it seemed forever but eventually the pain subsided and I was left as weak as a kitten. I lay on the ground for a long time before I could move, before I dared to move, in case the pain should return. Some of the lads wanted to help but nobody could. I just wanted to lie there and die.

Slowly regaining some sort of will to live I tried to diagnose the problem and wondered if I'd been poisoned. Well the Germans were adept at booby-traps, why not poison the bottled fruits; but it seemed unlikely. A more likely reason was colic and a pretty severe attack at that and I suppose living, or rather eating, as richly as I had done would be a good way to invite gut ache.

I went off bottled fruits but I still enjoyed ham and eggs, which reminds me. As I said before the hen house was cleared of eggs within minutes of arriving at farms but one day an advance party beat us to it. There on the hen house was a notice 'DO NOT TOUCH! THESE EGGS ARE FOR THE OFFICERS MESS!'. The notice was duly obeyed and the eggs were untouched. Within the next ten minutes however not one chicken was to be seen!

Steinhuder was a spa town on the shores of a very large lake, Steinhudermere, which was large enough to be a training ground for German E boats, the HQ of which I discovered was on an island in the middle of the lake. The main street ran roughly parallel to the lakeside but was separated from it by houses, hotels, shops and the shoreline. Arriving in the town, H Section was billeted in the attic floor of a main street hotel situated on the corner of a street running down to the lake. The hotel boasted a magnificent ground floor bar, bottle shelves lined with mirrors, and two very large 'cut-glass' chandeliers suspended from the ceiling. No staff or civilians in sight but lots of red berets, the owners of which proceeded to drink everything within sight.

It wasn't long before this was achieved and thus refreshed and halfway to being inebriated they set off to find that which was not in sight. In this 'Hunt the bottles' "Carter" and "Harris" were well to the fore. It wasn't long before a padlocked and chained metal trellis door leading to the cellar was found, and smashed open and down into the cellar they all went. Whatever they found they drank and came back to the bar clutching bottles. "Carter" and "Harris", now glassy eyed, staggered up with a dust-covered bottle containing a syrupy red liquid which, after enquiring of each other, "What the f's this?" drank it anyway. It was more than enough to smash them out of their minds and once the bottle was empty they sent it smashing into the mirrors at the back of the bar at the same time threatening to sexually assault the Germans! It was the signal for a free for all and the air was soon full of flying bottles, ash trays, chairs, etc. as the bar was systematically wrecked. Hollywood would have loved it! "Carter" and "Harris" now turned their attention to those lovely chandeliers and using chairs as weapons proceeded to reduce them to splinters of flying glass.

Ten minutes or so before this, someone, probably a civilian, shareholder or perhaps even the proprietor, seeing what was happening must have informed the authorities because - came the blast of a whistle and a stentorian voice bellowed, "Stand still the lot of you", and they did. There in the doorway stood the Provost Marshal himself flanked by four MPs. Everybody froze, "Carter" and "Harris" stood like statues, chairs still held aloft. The only thing moving were the chandeliers still swaying backwards and forwards and slowly losing momentum, the only sound was the tinkling of their pendant strands of shattered glass.

The Provost Marshal surveyed the scene for a moment defying anybody to twitch and then singling out "Carter" and "Harris" barked, "You two come with me. The rest of you clear this mess up." "Carter" and "Harris" followed the PM into the foyer. "Where are you billeted?", he barked.

"Up in the attic, Sir" came the reply.

"Right.", he said, "March up those stairs and if I see you so much as sway I'll put you both under open arrest. About turn, quick march."

"Carter" and "Harris" turned and side by side, just like a couple of guardsmen, they marched up those stairs. As they reached the top and the first landing the P.M. and MPs turned on their heels and left the Hotel. As they went out of the door, "Carter" and "Harris" also turned on their heels, involuntarily of course, and "Harris" hit every step as he came crashing down to the foyer. "Carter" collapsed in a heap on the landing. It was fortunate for them that we stopped at Steinhuder for a few days because Bill "Carter" was unconscious for 24 hours whilst Ken "Harris" was out for 3 nights and 2 days. Ken was like wax, his breathing extremely shallow, I thought he was dying. We laid him on his sleeping bag, covered him with a swastika flag, crossed his arms on his breast and placed a German helmet behind his head. The Section Officer came and had a look at him said, "He'll be alright", and shaking his head walked away.

Later on that same evening I went for a walk and look-see along the lakeshore. As I was admiring the view I could see a small rowing boat making for the shore, apparently having come from the island. There were two passengers only, one of whom was rowing. I watched them wide-eyed as they drew near. Both were in uniform - German Naval uniform - one more resplendent than the other.

They came ashore and marched towards me and the 'Admiral' said, "In the name of the Third Reich I surrender."

"You'd better come with me", I said and we set off along the shore. Approaching the turn-off for the town we were met by another of our lads, whom I didn't know, who said,

"What have you got there?"

"A German Admiral, I think", I said.

"Where are you taking him?", he asked.

"To the Provost Marshal", I replied. He then offered to take him off my hands and complete the job. As I had no idea where the P.M. was I thought it was a good idea and handed him over.

Many years afterwards, at the dinner table at the 'L'Oie Qui Fume' in Cabourg whilst on a D-Day Pilgrimage, Mike Hensman who was Adj. in 1945 was telling the story of how one of his chaps had brought in a German Admiral at Steinhuder. I immediately said, "That was me, Mike. I've often told my family that story." Mike looked at me, knowing it wasn't me that brought him in, and he changed the conversation. It took me a while to fathom out why at that moment I suddenly became 'Persona non grata'; You were right Mike, it was your bloke who brought him in and got the credit. But - and it's a true and big BUT - it was me who first picked him up and then handed him over to your chap! It's strange how chickens come home to roost!

Being in Steinhuder for a few days - well, "Harris" was still unconscious - we took to having a swim or two in the lake and oddly enough it was full of jellyfish which caused quite a lot of fun. I have a marvellous snap of Wally Petchey, with a peculiar expression on his face, sticking his hand down the front of his swimming trunks trying to dislodge what he called, "one of those jelly-bleeders." Happy memories indeed!

#19   Ted and Wally Petchy at Steinhuder in April 1945
Wally is having some difficulty extracting a jellyfish from his swimming trunks!

We moved on past columns of German prisoners and now past hundreds of refugees pushing handcarts laden with household goods, blankets, clothing etc. It's possible they were from forced labour camps and were on their way to transit camps before going home. At one time they were so numerous that I was driving with two wheels in the ditch and two on the roadside. In one big town we reached, Osnabruch, the population were being temporarily evicted from their homes in order to facilitate billeting of troops. As I pulled in to the kerbside and stopped, a woman detached herself from the crowd, who, carrying personal belongings, were being evicted. She came over to me and said in faultless English and with tears streaming down her face, "I did not think the British would do this to us."

I looked at her for a moment and remembering what the Germans had done to others and by comparison she had nothing to cry about said, "Well we are, on your way."

That night I slept in a German officer's house who must have had something to do with Nazi propaganda. His cupboards and bookcase were full of books, leaflets, pictures etc. I brought home a set of photos of the 1936 Berlin Olympic Games, a Hitler in Paris book, a Naval book and a music book and I still have them.

A forced labour camp had been liberated close by and the Dutch, French, Belgian etc. ex-slaves were loose in the town picking up as much as they could carry en route for home. Some of them came into the house we were in and their priority was blankets and clothing shoes etc. We let them help themselves. One of them was a Dutch lad and I showed him the song Willy had given me 'Warrom Wou Jy' and said "That is Dutch." Full of euphoria at being released and full of hate for the Germans he took the card with the Dutch words on and said "Deutch, Deutch" and ripped it in two. Sadly I picked up the pieces and he went on his way rejoicing. I had those words for a long time and thought they had somehow or other got lost. But no! Happily they had just been misplaced and in the year 2003, 58 years later, I found them and here they are:

"WAARROM WOU JY VAN MY NOCH VAN MYN LIEF DE WETEN

WAARROM LIEP JY MY ALS EEN VREEMDE STEEDS VOORBY

DAT IK JOU LIEF HEB KON JE DAT ZO MAAR VERGETEN

IK HOU ALLEEN NOG MAAR VAN EEN EN DAT BEN JY"

which, roughly translated, means:

Why did you ignore me and my love?

Why did you pass me like a stranger?

The way I love you how can you forget

That there's only one thing I love and that's you

Shortly after that a French ex-slave came in frantically trying to make himself understood and I found myself being obliged to try and make some sense of his story. When I finally managed to calm him down and got him to speak slowly I discovered that one of the prison guards, a right Nazi swine apparently, had donned civilian clothes and was now abroad in the town hoping to go undetected, but this prisoner had seen him and recognized him and was intent on catching him. I took him along to the Provost Marshall's office and told his story. A couple of MPs, the ex-prisoner and myself walked the town until at last the Nazi was spotted.

"You can leave this to us now" said the MPs. No medal, no commendation, not even a well done or a thank you. They didn't even ask for my name, rank and number but I didn't half make that Frenchman happy and that in itself was enough!

Was it also in this town that we opened a huge creamery to the 'slaves'? Even the civilians joined the rush and carried away gallons of milk etc.

Oh! I also brought home from that officer's house his sword and uniform and a huge Nazi flag. The moths got the uniform, my wife made cushion covers from the flag, but I still have the sword.

On we went and late April found us close to the last barrier before the Baltic, the River Elbe. Apparently we were to be visited by Monty very soon so we had to smarten ourselves up a bit. I think also that Monty was going to dish some gongs out. Not however to me. In view of this the CO held a preliminary parade, took one look at me and nearly had a fit. I can't honestly say that I blamed him. I was filthy. My battledress was much closer to black than khaki and my trousers weren't much better. What else could he expect! Humping and charging batteries, maintaining a jeep and spilling sulphuric acid over everything tends to turn things black. Not to mention crawling around ditches, forests, pigsties, hen-houses and cellars.

Having established that I only had the one uniform I was told to draw a five- gallon can of petrol and get my uniform cleaned. I had a willing helper in a P.O.W. and we found an old tin bath and got to work. Even after 'possing' and changing the petrol a gallon at a time it was still turning black. What was I wearing during this laundry session? An old pair of denims someone found for me. It cost the army another can of petrol before my uniform began to look more like khaki than black and I wrang it out and hung it on a line in the farmyard to dry out.

Next day, on parade and inspection by the Colonel closely followed by the Section Officer, the Colonel stopped in front of me as I stood stiffly and proudly to attention, looked me up and down and said, "Your uniform's rather grubby, get some petrol and have it cleaned!!" Every fibre in my body wanted to explode into uncontrollable laughter, I hadn't heard anything so funny for years. Over the Colonel's shoulders the Section Officer stood glaring at me and I could hear the message loud and clear that those eyes were drilling into me, "Don't you bloody dare!" Such is Army discipline that I didn't bloody dare, much as I wanted to, it was so hilarious - I just looked straight ahead and without even the ghost of a smile answered, "Yes, Sir."

The inspection over and the presentation of medals completed, out of my sight as it happened, Montgomery then launched into one of his 'morale' speeches. The gist of it being that everything was going very well and that he was always interested to see what the papers had to say.

"I read," he said, "that Monty is on the banks of the Elbe and that they wouldn't be surprised if he was across tomorrow."

"Gentlemen", he said, "neither would I. In fact I wouldn't be surprised if I was across tonight." Then, "Good hunting", or "Knock them for six", or something like that.

He was, and we were, and on to Luneberg. En route we met a horde of refugees and prisoners. The refugees I learnt later were German civilians, fleeing from the Russians who were rapidly advancing towards Wismar and Lubeck, looting, raping and pillaging as they went. The German civilians were running for their lives. Once again we were in a farm and quite a large one with lots of buildings and barns and quite a few German soldiers only too eager to lend a hand. They looked like old men and some had lost fingers and toes due to frostbite on the Russian front. They were harmless and we let them potter around and fetch and carry.

Chapter 14   Victory in Europe

There was now no doubt, nor had there ever been since we crossed the Rhine, that it was just a matter of time. Now it was just a matter of days and we were becoming more and more euphoric as we got nearer to the Baltic, to Wismar, and to the end of war with Germany. We got to Wismar on the 6th May and Germany surrendered on 8th May. The war was over but some Germans wouldn't accept the fact and took to shooting at us in the streets of Wismar. They were nicknamed 'Werewolves' and armed patrols were out on the streets night and day to combat them. One was even dumped on the pavement outside the Town Hall just as he'd been shot and a notice put by his bloodied body warning the townspeople to expect no mercy if they persisted. I have a picture of that.

#20   A dead 'Werewolf' outside Wismar Town Hall in May 1945

A portrait of Adolf Hitler is propped up against a box next to the body

We were billeted in a detached house in Wismar, Derek Hogarth and I occupying a bedroom on the top floor. One day as a bunch of us was lounging around outside, Derek turned up, eyes shining, and said,

"If you can guess what I've found you can have it."

"Oh!", I said, "a top hat."

Derek's face was a picture. "How did you know that?" he said.

21   The Wismar billet

After all these years Derek, I'll tell you! I could recognise a folded 'opera hat' anywhere and I'd spotted it as you came out of the house! I have a photo of a group in which I am wearing a top hat and that's how I came by it. I also have one or two pictures of us having 'high jinks' in German uniforms, Jim Crotty, Tommy Grant and myself.

22   Ted wearing the top hat

23   Ted, Jim Crotty and Tommy Grant in German uniform

24   More "High Jinks" at Wismar

We spent the next week or so revelling in the end of the war and the relief of not being shot at, shelled or mortared anymore. We'd survived and life was sweet. The 'Werewolves' were just a nuisance, albeit a dangerous one. It is difficult to describe the great feeling of peaceful joy now that it was all over and we were the victors, but it was reflected in everything we did, said or thought and shone from every face we looked at. It was with this kind of feeling that I set off in my jeep with someone I've totally forgotten, to meet the Russians. Down to the Baltic coast road we went and turned right, half a mile further along to the East and there they were. Across the road was a pole barrier - a forerunner of the iron curtain!! - flanked by two of the scruffiest soldiers I've ever seen - even including me on the Elbe. Baggy blouses and baggy pants tucked into calf-length boots and armed with vicious looking automatic weapons. We climbed out of the jeep and approached them not knowing what sort of a reception we'd get. It was broad grins all round, backslapping and a totally reciprocally unintelligible Russian/English conversation. Oddly enough it was two or three German words that cemented the camaraderie – "Deutsche Kaput! Alles Kaput!" At last we understood each other!

While this was going on, down the road from the Russian side came a big lorry. When it stopped a huge Russian officer, immaculately dressed, chest full of real medals, got out of the cab, went round to the rear, barked an order and came over to us followed by another two Russians carrying a five gallon jerry can, armsful of crockery and God knows what else. More backslapping, handshaking, Anglo/Russian gobbledygook, "Deutsche Kaput, Alles Kaput", interspersed with laughter followed.

A snap of the fingers and the contents of the jerry can was decanted into a delicate china bowl and from there into delicate china cups, they could well have been Dresden, and looked under the circumstances totally incongruous. Loot of course.

Another snap of the fingers and the 'God knows what else' turned out to be a large loaf of black bread and a roll of, and I'm sure it was, raw bacon! Cradling them one at a time, under his left arm, the officer hacked off bite-size chunks with a vicious looking knife and handed them round. Unsure what to do next, I watched and waited. Into the Russian's mouths went the bread and bacon and not wishing to let the British Army down I did likewise. If the bacon wasn't raw it tasted like it - YUK! But down it went. Then it was china cup time and with the toast "Nastrovia" or something like that, down went the vodka!

More backslapping etc followed and then it was a repeat performance. This time, however, I palmed the bacon and when it came to "Nastrovia" and all the heads were tipped back - because it went down in one - I slung the bacon over my left shoulder. It worked like a charm and so did the next two or three "Nastrovias". Then the Russians, but not the sentries, had to leave and with many more handshakes and backslapping it was "Dosti Vanya" and off they went.

As it was also time we made tracks, we returned to the jeep and I climbed into the driver's seat and sat looking at the road. I knew it was a straight, hard, tarmac road; my brain told me that. The only trouble was, my eyes told a different story. Try as I may I just couldn't get it to stand still. In a gentle, slow motion it moved to the left and then to the right and then it split into two roads which moved in opposite directions, occasionally crossing each other. Not only that, it was also slowly undulating at the same time like the gentle ripples on a pond or a child's skipping rope held at one end and shaken up and down at the other. It was beautiful, fascinating and hypnotic. I had enough sense to realise it was also impossible; roads just don't do that. I also had enough sense to say to my passengers, "Can you drive? - because I bloody can't."

The jeep pulled up at the door and I was helped along the path, through the door, up the stairs and into the bedroom. God knows what I looked like - stupid I should imagine - but Derek stood looking at me wide-eyed and open-mouthed, that much I remember, then I said, "Hello Derek, I've never been so pissed in all my life", and I passed out and fell face down on the bed.

It would be about 2 p.m. I heard later that the word got around and that the lads came to see for themselves if it was true. The general concensus of opinion was one of disbelief. "We didn't think he drank like that." Well they were absolutely right - I didn't!

At seven o' clock I was woken up, I was on patrol! Out into the streets of Wismar with no ill effects at all, no headache, no hangover. Oddly enough there was one beneficial effect. It was night-time and it was dark but my pupils were so dilated they took in every scrap of light there was and I found I could see the whole length of a street. Happy in the knowledge that I would see them before they saw me I continued and concluded an uneventful tour of duty.

Towards the end of May the 6th A/B Div. were ordered back to England and we set off from Wismar on the Baltic en route for Ostend and the Channel. The weather was glorious, so much so that, travelling slowly as convoys do, I found myself nodding at the wheel and in danger of colliding with the vehicle in front. How the opportunity presented itself I have forgotten but I swapped my jeep for a DR's bike and set off in glorious sunshine to roar up and down the autobahn free from the restrictions of convoy discipline. The last time I had ridden a motor bike was in the Ardennes under adverse conditions. Here in the sunshine, I was having a great time. It didn't last long however and I was 'obliged' by the Military Police to rejoin the convoy. At 5 m.p.h. it wasn't long before I fell asleep and finished up in the ditch. I went back to my jeep, it was much safer.

Sometimes convoys halted for no apparent reason. If you were in the front, of course, you had a chance to find out why, otherwise you stood still, sometimes for a very long time and were left wondering. On one such occasion we stopped in the countryside - nothing but miles and miles of fields, hedges and trees with this one exception. One solitary but very large building, stuck in the middle of the fields. No village, no houses, nothing, just this very large building, most puzzling!

Of course it was investigated and proved to be a glass factory and backwards and forwards went the lads with their loads of glass cups, saucers, plates and bowls. Off I went, not having yet set up home, and loaded with a crate of dinner and tea set and a half dozen assorted bowls and plenty of straw for packing I staggered back with this load and was just piling them on my jeep when - just my luck - the Section Officer turned up.

"What have you got there?", he asked, so I told him.

"That's looting", he said, "put it back."

I was thinking 'spoils of war' but no, it was looting and back I had to go. It was even heavier on the return journey, at least a quarter of a mile across the open fields and I went back into the factory and said to myself, "Well if I can't have it neither can anybody else", and I dropped it with a resounding and satisfactory crash. I hadn't cared much for Captain Hamer since he made me ride his bike into the Ardennes. I cared for him even less at that moment even though he was right and was doing his duty.

 # 25   Ted enjoying 'Victory in Europe' near Luneburg in May 1945

I can only recall two overnight stops en route for Ostend and the first was just north of Brussels and we spent the night in a hayloft in the centre of the floor of which was an open trap door. As the whole floor was covered in hay we did not know the trap door existed - well, not until somebody fell through and I thought here we go again, just like George Atkinson in Panningen. This time nobody could save this poor chap but he fell softly on a pile of hay below. Also, this time, we knew better than to light a fire!

Brussels was so close that we thought we'd like to visit it. Some for cultural and educational reasons - the liars - others for a pint. "Carter" and "Harris", of course, for 'les girls'. Accordingly we asked for and were granted a few hours leave and a 'passion wagon', i.e. transport, and off we went. Culture and education were out, as it was night-time almost everything was closed and lighting was almost non-existent. One place which was lit turned out to be a shop selling cosmetics etc. I was able to buy for my wife a miniature compact containing block powder; a lip-stick and a small bottle of perfume called Blue Narcissus. The idea of bringing presents home from the war appealed to me.

We wandered around until, down a side street, we spotted a neon sign. Like bees to the hive we swarmed and found ourselves in a tiny nightclub with a bar on the left and a band and a few girls at the bottom end. We ordered 'biere' and got a shock when the bill arrived and they got a shock when we left so abruptly. With various cries of, "Bloody hell!", "God almighty!", and other such exclamations we set off anew to seek further sustenance and found a cafe on a street corner.

This was more like it, well-lit and reasonable prices and at the bar one or two of 'les girls' with smashing figures; from behind. When they turned round, however, and came to our table with, "Allo Tommee", it should have been 'les grandmeres'. Bill "Carter", however, was undeterred; shades of, "Is your Granny in?", and was only too keen to prove his virility. There was only one snag, he didn't have enough money. He was so disappointed and pleaded with us so desperately that we took pity on him and had a whip round to send him happily upstairs into the arms of his 'Grandmere' and into the brothel which, until that moment, we hadn't known existed. Two beers later he returned and we set off to find our, on this occasion at least for "Carter", truly named 'passion wagon'.

As we roared through the 'Grand Place' of Brussels we passed a Military Policeman directing traffic and as we sped by from every throat in the back of the lorry came the old battle cry, "All coppers are bastards." As we disappeared into the gloom the MP turned to his bike parked nearby, kick started it and took off in hot pursuit. Despite pleas to our driver to get his bloody foot down we were overhauled and stopped. Round to the back of the lorry came the MP and to our amazement he was an officer. An officer directing traffic? He then proceeded to give us a right bollicking.

"Bloody Airborne! I might have known! Think you won the bloody war all by yourself don't you! Big headed lot of bastards" etc. By the time he'd finished 'dressing us down' and I must say my recollection is that he did it very well, we felt a lot more humble. We apologised and pleaded high spirits and as he roared back to Brussels I could imagine him with a big grin on his face thinking, "That sorted those buggers out!"

The next stop I recall was not too far from the coast and Ostend and within driving distance of Bruges and therefore of Steenbrugge which was a suburb. A friend of my wife's mother was a lady named Maud who lived in Chester-le-Street, Co Durham. 'Aunt Maud', as she was known, had a sister named Sal who had married a Belgian during the First World War. This 'Aunt Sal' had brought up a family of four girls and a boy and she lived in Lopphemstratte, Steenbrugge. Her husband worked on the Belgian Railway. Throughout the war and occupation no one gave her away and the Germans never found out that she was an Englishwoman. Apart from the odd contact via the Red Cross no direct contact had been possible from England until now.

I approached the Section Officer, told him the story, convinced him it was true with the aid of a letter from home asking me to look them up if possible, and asked for permission to take my jeep and go and find them. It was given, providing I was back by midnight and took a passenger. I mentally forgave Hamer for the Ardennes and the glassware. Without maps and road signs I managed to find Steenbrugge. I think it must have been by stopping and asking.

Whatever; here I am at the top of a street in Steenbrugge waiting to ask my way from a young girl who is walking up the street in my direction.

"Excuse me please, can you tell me where Lopphemstratte is?"

"This is Lopphemstratte.", she replied in pretty good English, "Who do you look for?"

"Van Quathem", I replied.

"I am Van Quathem", she said wide-eyed.

"I'm looking for Aunt Sal", I said, "I'm Ted from England."

She let out a big yell, turned on her heels and flew down the street and into a house on the left hand side.

A few moments later a group of girls came galloping out and practically carried me into the house and into the arms of Aunt Sal. It was, of course, the first time I had seen any of them - Aunt Sal or her daughters. Out came the wine and biscuits and then we had to eat with them and no way would they let me go that night. I had to give them all the news and answer hundreds of questions and they put us to bed, up the ladders and into the attic. I didn't sleep that night. Two things kept me awake. First, the close proximity of the four girls, and second, facing Hamer the next morning. I was, no matter how I looked at it, A.W.O.L. I much preferred however to think of the girls and, at the same time, keep an eye on my passenger in case he took it into his head to creep downstairs.

Early next morning I said my goodbyes and set off to find the Div. They were all ready to move and George Atkinson, who had been promoted to Sergeant in place of Bowkett, was doing his nut. Somehow or other he had covered for me when my absence was noticed; well, we'd gone through the war together. I told him I'd had a puncture and had to wait till first light to change the wheel. He knew it was less than the truth but he also knew it was a reasonable excuse should any awkward questions be asked later. Fortunately all went well.

On the dockside at Ostend, German cars were being sold to the locals for a song, souvenirs and even army blankets were being flogged and how they got away with it I'll never know.

Back in England we had to go through Customs, "Anything to declare?" Kit bags and small and big packs examined and punched! God knows what they thought we had. No duty free in those days and we hadn't exactly been on holiday. While all this was going on I could see the Engineers lorries going through with three or four E boats lashed and tarpaulined in the back or were they just speed boats? Whatever, somebody was going to be well off. Maybe it was official, maybe! Anyway, what the hell, we'd just won the war and I'm on my way home!

Home once more, on leave, and basking in the euphoria of a great victory. No more raids and bombs. No more shot and shell. Life was sweet and no longer in danger - or was it? Back to barracks and once again the task of re-equipping. I remember Cpl. Hamer dumping a German radio set in front of me one day and saying,

"See if you can strip that, but do it carefully. I'll be back later." And off he went. The set was held in a protective casing by about 10 or 12 screws. I duly undid them, slid the set out of the case and awaited his return.

"No problem?" he asked.

"None Sir", I said, "but why had I to be careful?"

"Because", he said, "sometimes these sets have been booby trapped"!!!

No longer in danger? Well that's what I thought.

Ominously we were issued with string vests - holes tied up with string - but amazingly enough they were to prove very warm at night. Advance parties were shipped off to foreign parts and the buzz went round that somehow and somewhere we were to be involved with the Japs. Somehow or other I hadn't bargained for that! Before, however, anything else could happen the Yanks dropped the atom bomb. The what? Well it was news to us then and very welcome news too because it put an end to the Japanese war and any necessity for us to be involved. I was, later on, to be doubly thankful when I learned that we had been scheduled for an Airborne Drop on Singapore!

Chapter 15   The State of Emergency

Hip-hip! Now the war is really over and I can look forward to demob. After all I only joined for the duration of the war didn't I? Well - no! It seemed that I, and a few thousand more, had also joined for – 'during the state of emergency'!! - and they'd found one in PALESTINE! Which emergency soon found me leaning over the rail of 'The Arundel Castle' in the Mersey, the Liver Building behind me, gazing wistfully over to Wallasey and saying to the chap next to me, "And to think I only live a couple of hundred miles from here."

To which he replied, "You should worry, I can almost see my bloody house from here", and with those sad thoughts we set sail for the 'Holy Land'!

Holy Land? I was about to have my choirboy visions and beliefs rudely shattered and it set me looking for the truth, a quest which I still pursue by devouring every archaeological and literary discovery available. For the moment, however, here I am bound for an alien, albeit Holy, land - aboard a troop ship. Below decks were stripped of cabins, corridors etc. and in their place were acres of hammocks slung between iron stanchions, pillars and what-have-you. It was quite a trick climbing in and out of a hammock but we soon learned. A tannoy system kept everyone informed of what or who was required and where and when at all hours. The opening words of which announcement never varied, "D'yer hear there, d'yer hear there." I had the misfortune to have one of the loudspeakers, and I do mean LOUD speakers, adjacent to my hammock. Once the initial shock had passed however I grew accustomed to the routine. The queue for meals wound three or four times round the deck before you eventually reached the galley and the waiting was quite a bind but once again it became part of life.

We sailed some time in September and, as I recall, the weather was pretty decent until about 2 a.m. one morning when, whilst everyone below decks was asleep, we sailed into a storm whilst skirting the Bay of Biscay. We were all made aware of the situation because it was at that precise moment that the ship, I think the term is 'yawed', violently, the hammocks did an up and over and we were unceremoniously dumped on the deck. It wasn't exactly 'panic stations' but the one thought uppermost in everyone's mind was, "What the hell's going on? Torpedoes?" We soon knew.

The ship continued to yaw, heave, rock, roll, stand on its prow and judder as the screw left the water. To us landlubbers it was pretty frightening, to the crew it was probably a bit rough. Hundreds were immediately sea-sick and poor Derek Hogarth turned green and crouched in the corner of a bulkhead and stayed there for two days slowly dying. On deck the queue for meals was instantly halved, on the second day halved again and on the third day when the storm was just a 'heavy swell' only a handful of us went for breakfast. It happened to be stewed liver and as I was going in to the galley someone came out carrying his dinner tray and, as he passed me, momentarily paused, gagged and brought his breakfast up all over his tray right under my nose. I suddenly lost my appetite. That was the only meal I missed but I wasn't sick once. I must have an 'old salt's' gene somewhere in my makeup!

By now Derek Hogarth was beginning to worry us, he was still below decks and was now a very unhealthy looking yellow. We decide he needed fresh air and, although all previous attempts to move him had failed, on this occasion we succeeded in getting him on deck. There we stood at the rail hanging on to Derek keeping him upright and trying to persuade him to eat something - well he hadn't had a thing for three days. Finally we bullied him into eating half an orange, a slice at a time. After all fruit is good for you isn't it? Not for him however, it was no sooner down than it was up and all over the deck. As the days went by and the weather improved he slowly came back into the land of the living.

Once we got past the storm it was plain sailing or rather steaming. Life on board was idyllic, no duties of any sort, no guards, no pickets, no swabbing decks, which reminds me. As the weather improved, life below decks got very hot and some of us took to sleeping on deck, but not for long. Decks were swabbed regularly and after the first attempt to wash us into the bilges, or worse still overboard, we gave up and stayed below at nights.

It was generally agreed that somehow or other Sgt. Major Carr had managed to get the Signals excused duty but whoever or however we were very grateful. During those idyllic summer days sailing through the Med. life on board was heaven. Huge kettles of tea and biscuits could be bought from the galley and resold among the lads. Housey-housey, Crown & Anchor, card and domino schools abounded and the ship's crew ran a daily 'Guess how far we've travelled' lottery. I remember some of the lads staying awake all night on occasions just to hear if the rev of the ship's engines increased - great fun!

Sailing very close to Gibraltar was a thrill and spotting the tiny rocky island of Pantalleria an added bonus, as was the sight of dolphins and the occasional school of flying fish! On all these memorable moments the ship's rail and every other vantage point was crowded with bodies all straining to get a good view and none more so than when the smoking cone of Mount Etna came into view. Not exactly luxurious but nevertheless a Mediterranean Cruise and all free. Glorious sunshine, blue skies, blue sea, free board and lodgings and after the tumult and fire of the war - we were at peace and out of danger - almost. There were still some German U-boats at large. Fortunately none came our way and with the pungent sickly smell of Africa in our nostrils we sailed on to finally drop anchor off Haifa about 10 days after we'd left Liverpool. Our holiday cruise was over and it was now back to work!!!

 # 26   The Arundel Castle viewed from a barge in Haifa Bay 24/09/1945

As Haifa had no deep-water harbour we were ferried ashore in smaller craft and landed on the quayside adjacent to the railway. We were then loaded onto trucks, large empty trucks with large sliding doors similar to the ones the Germans used to transport the Jews to the death camps. There would be about twenty of us to a truck, not one seat between us but at least we could lie down on the floor and stretch out. Doors closed and we settled down for the long overnight journey the length of Palestine to arrive very early the following morning at Nuseirat Ridge near Gaza - the notorious Gaza Strip!

 # 27   On board the Haifa to Deir-el-Balah cattle truck

At Nuseirat there had been a hospital and the buildings were utilised as Admin. offices. For the rest of us it was a case of unloading two trainloads of gear and erecting bell-tents and marquees. Mad dogs and Englishmen, and on this occasion the 6th A/B Div., go out in the mid-day sun. We sweated for two days but the camp took shape and became habitable. One of the first things we did was to dig latrines - two holes in the sand! One, for the officers, had a small bottomless dustbin surmounted by a toilet seat with a lid fitted over the hole and was screened by a hessian on sticks wall. The 'Other Ranks' bog was similar but minus lid and was also hessian screened. On the very first evening, and there was hardly any dusk before it was dark, someone 'en passant' asked, "Where's the bog?" He was directed and off he set. He was back very soon saying he couldn't find it. He was re-directed and when he returned once more unsuccessful, with many ribald comments it was decided to hold his hand and take him to the toilets. We couldn't find them either, but we did find the two holes in the sand. We'd been there less than a day and the locals had struck - they'd pinched our bogs! The 'Wogs' had our Bogs! That was the start and they continued their thieving ways until my last day in the Middle East eight months later. Nothing was safe and 24-hour alertness became a way of life, and in the case of the Jewish terrorist groups, of life and death.

Two days of hard labour under a blazing sun and we were ready for a rest, but no way. "You will now dig trenches around the tents."

"What the hell for?", we wanted to know.

"Storm drains", was the reply!!

"Storm drains??", we said; "in this blazing climate? You must be joking!"

"No joke; get digging." It was another case of 'Mad dogs' etc. and we duly dug. Much later on when eventually the rain did come it ran off the tents in streams and ran down the overflowing storm drains in raging torrents to disappear into the sand away from the tent lines. Somebody knew more than we did and as it kept us dry we were very grateful for it.

Once we were nicely settled in at Nuseirat and we were able to 'look around' we discovered that just over the sand dunes about half a mile away was the Mediterranean. Duty permitting, it became a regular feature of life - into the Med. The water was warm and the breakers huge and we had a lot of fun diving through them. Once however I mistimed my dive and was flattened by the wave and scrubbed ashore on the bottom of the sea. It was like a huge hand holding me down and I was totally helpless and pretty badly scratched about the chest, arms and legs, from the gritty sand. Needless to say I had a healthy respect for the Med. after that. Our daily bathe was soon noticed by one enterprising Arab who turned up one day on his camel and proceeded to try to sell us dates, figs, jaffas, grapefruit, watches, carpets, etc., etc. It was quite exotic! Not long after that an order was posted forbidding us to buy from these itinerant traders - hygienically unsafe!

En route across the dunes and scrub to the beach one day I noticed small cairns of stones dotted about the place. At first I thought they might be old graves but as these were so few and so far apart I decided they couldn't be and gave up trying to work out what on earth they could be. I found out in the most unexpected manner. Negotiating this 'graveyard' I chanced on a small tree about 6 feet tall, one of about a dozen scattered about the place. It was a pretty bare tree but my attention was drawn to an appendage hanging down from one of the branches and then I saw a few more hanging from other branches. I stood for a while trying to decide what I was looking at and a glimmer of an idea began to form. Could it be? I plucked one and split it open, smelled and tasted it. It was! I had seen and tasted for the first time in my life a fresh wild fig.

"Come on, hurry up", came from one of the lads ahead of me, and then, "What are you doing?"

"Look what I've found I replied", and soon we started to tuck in. The figs were delicious but they were not wild, far from it. What was wild, however, was the Palestinian who appeared on the horizon, doing a war dance and yelling his head off. The small cairns of stones dotted around the sand were the boundary of his 'garden'!

Splashing around in the Med. shortly after that incident I couldn't help thinking, "They pinched our bog and we pinched their figs! There must be a connection there somewhere."

Speaking of bogs reminds me. In one part of the old hospital site, and quite some distance from the Admin. buildings, was a permanent bog. Imagine if you will a cylindrical shaft sunk to a depth of some 40 feet or so and capped by a circular 3 foot thick concrete collar of about 10 feet diameter through which had been drilled holes, which, in turn, were rimmed by wooden rings. Each 'toilet seat' was separated from its neighbour by a wooden wall like the spokes of a wheel and the whole edifice surrounded by a wall which safeguarded the modesty of those inside. Being, unlike the 'netties' from my childhood, unemptyable, the contents were covered from time to time with lime. The smell was such that no-one lingered long; especially in those few moments between dusk and dark because it was then that the creepy crawlies surfaced and the sight of a 12 inch long, half inch thick, centipede, millipede, or in my case trillipede, wending its leg-rippling way towards me was enough to 'up pants' and off P.D.Q.

The wild life in Palestine, apart from the natives, was fascinating. Camels and donkeys although not really wild were left to graze in the scrub and against a background of palm trees looked quite exotic and biblical. Spiders as big as golfballs I could do without, as I could scorpions, but gekkos were absolutely delightful. They were like miniature prehistoric monsters and could run very fast and go up a perpendicular wall with the greatest of ease. Having one in your tent was a Godsend as they made short work of insects and flies besides keeping you entertained. The other really wild life were the wild dogs, pi-dogs, which roamed and hunted or scavenged in packs and were very dangerous, especially so being rabid. But more of them later.

Everybody in Africa or the Middle East wore K.D. i.e. Khaki Drill, a sand coloured lightweight uniform issued with short and long trousers. We also had normal battledress most essential for night-time guard duty. In stark contrast to the blazing hot days the nights were bitterly cold and wrapping up was essential. About the only pleasure I could find in night guard duty were the brilliant stars against the black sky, quite beautiful, as was the moon. But it was cold. As the weeks went by Arab dhobi wallahs; laundry men; appeared and for a few mils or the odd piastre your uniform would be cleaned and pressed and returned like new with creases you could almost shave with. The return one morning of my pristine K.D. coincided with one of my turns 'on guard'.

On this occasion we were being inspected by R.S.M. Carr and after he had walked up and down the row of men standing rigidly to attention he came back to me and tapping me on the shoulder with his baton said, "This one."

"Oh! my God", I thought, "what have I done wrong? My uniform is straight from the laundry, my boots are shining bright, my webbing is newly blancoed, my brasses are bright, I'm washed and shaved. What the hell is wrong?"

His next words didn't help the situation either, "You've got the stick."

Not having heard the expression before I had no idea what he meant but he didn't seem to be in a particularly bad mood so I ventured, "What does that mean Sergeant Major?"

"It means", he said, "You are the smartest man on parade and you are excused guard duty now or on some future occasion! Which is it to be?"

In a matter of milliseconds I thought, "Strike while the iron is hot. A bird in the hand is worth two in the bush. Now you lucky so-and-so now!"

"Now Sah", I said.

"Right, fall out", said R.S.M. Carr, with which order I gladly complied and went on my way rejoicing and blessing all good dhobi wallahs.

#28   "You've got the stick!"

Ted in khaki drill. October 1945

Back in my tent I stripped off my beautiful K.D. and carefully folded it until needed again. Reclining on my bed musing on my good fortune, and basking in the improbability of being complimented by R.S.M. Carr, I was rudely interrupted by one of the lads bursting into my tent and my reverie wanting to borrow my uniform as he'd been nobbled for guard duty in my place. Feeling totally at peace with the world I told him to piss off.

I can't remember when, probably November, but eventually we moved to a high security camp near the village of Bir Jaacov. Ten-foot high barbed wire perimeter fence strung on iron stanchions with battery operated jeep headlights mounted on tripods acting as searchlights. The guards had a roving commission at all times with access to 'search lights for night' scanning. Even so, one morning it was discovered that an empty marquee, which had been adjacent to another marquee housing Military Police, had vanished! 'Consternation in the Camp' was putting it mildly. Thank God it didn't happen when I was on guard. It appears that the fence had been cut, the guy ropes had been cut, the marquee lowered and tied up then tied to a camel which had dragged it out into the scrub to a nearby clump of palm trees where the thieves were waiting. Having so far been undetected they then disappeared with the camel and marquee into the night. Despite roving guards and searchlights nothing had been seen or heard!!

Another incident I recall was heard. A 'clank' of metal on metal, to be precise, alerted the guard. The next faint 'clank' came after a long pause and helped to give a clue to the general direction of the noise and the 'searchlight' was switched on. Caught in the beam was a native loading yet another iron stanchion on his donkey. A couple of hops, skip and a jump and the thief was out of the beam and he disappeared into the darkness leaving behind him a large gap in the fence and a donkey slowly going bow-legged with the weight. The wires of course having been cut from each stanchion. The sequel was quite amusing. The donkey was impounded and the owner traced; he naturally was not at home so his wife and household goods were also impounded. It seemed reasonable to assume that he would return to claim them. They were housed and fed for quite a few days before the penny dropped and they were released. Not for nothing were they called Wily Oriental Gentlemen!

Another story which was 'doing the rounds' at this time concerned the silent dismantling and disappearance of a 25 pounder gun albeit, fortunately, from some other camp. Considering the size and weight of such a gun, that it should have vanished unheard and unseen only added to the legendary thieving abilities of the indigenous population.

It was about this time that a notice was posted up on the Camp information board which had me puzzled. It said, in effect, that you must not fire on anyone unless they had got inside the camp perimeter! I was discussing this with some of the lads when the R.S.M strolled up.

"What's the problem?", he asked.

"According to this notice", I replied, "a bunch of terrorists could stand outside the fence and shoot at us and we could do nothing about it."

"Who told you that?", he barked! "Shoot the bastards, then drag them inside", and off he strode, a big grin on his face and leaving me feeling very stupid.

Chapter 16　　　Crazy Antics

It was in November 1945 that the 6th Airborne Div. Stage Club was formed. Its first objective being to put out a concert at Christmas. The chairman was Lieutenant R.G. Smith, the producer Signalman Dick Le Jeune, and Private Stephenson, RAMC, was secretary. Auditions were held, the cast chosen and rehearsals started. The first two shows were given on Christmas Eve and Christmas Day in the cinema of 12 General Hospital.

Weeks before Christmas 1945 we had been buying dozens of bottles of beer and every conceivable bottle of spirits you can think of. We had the lot. All Jewish distilled of course. It was one of the wonders of the world! After years of war, deprivation and blackout we were now in the land of plenty, overflowing with milk and honey and everything else that money could buy. Booze, food, wine, fruit, meat, vegetables, shoes, clothes etc., etc. and not a coupon in sight, no ration books, no queues and the whole place was lit up! Whatever you wanted you could buy. Shop windows crowded with merchandise, colourful, glittering and tempting. To blacked-out, deprived and rationed Britons it was truly Aladdin's Cave. I talk chiefly of course about New Jerusalem and Tel Aviv. Old Jerusalem and the Arab towns were mostly Bazaars and 'Hole-in-the-wall' market type shops - colourful nevertheless and fascinating.

But back to Xmas 1945. After Xmas dinner the tables stretching the length of the marquee were filled with bottles and the benches with bodies. After a few hours of 'straight' drinks someone decided to mix cocktails and to that end pressed into service Airborne flasks. In went generous helpings of various kinds of booze, shaken with freshly squeezed orange, grapefruit, lemon or what have you. It was then tested for taste and topped up with whatever took the fancy. I just vaguely remember a head coming round the marquee and surveying the scene some hours later. Most had fallen head forward onto the tables, some had fallen off the benches and some were under the tables. One or two were still sitting precariously on the benches. Being one of the latter I turned at the sound of my name being called, "Has anyone seen Ted Hold?", and promptly fell off the bench at the same time saying, "Come and have a drink."

"Jesus Christ", said this other voice, "You're singing at 7 o'clock." I was grabbed, stuffed into the back of a lorry and whizzed off to I didn't know where. I was then unceremoniously bundled off the lorry and frog marched round the back of a building where I was stripped to the waist and my head forcibly held under a tap in the wall which was gushing forth ice cold water on the nape of my neck, head, face and mouth. Just as I was beginning to think, "The buggers are trying to drown me" I was stood upright and a cup of hot black coffee poured down my throat. It was then back under the tap for further soakings. After about four or five cups of coffee and soakings I was pronounced sober enough to perform and I was duly dried, dressed, made to look presentable and bunged on the stage at 12 General Hospital in front of a packed house and I sang like Caruso! Well! I thought I did!!! Happy Xmas 1945!!!

The highlight of my sojourn in Palestine I nearly didn't have! Passing someone one day he stopped me and said, "I thought you would be at Jerusalem with the concert party." On asking why, I discovered they'd all gone off to Radio Station JCPA (Jerusalem Central Palestine Area) to be auditioned by The Forces Broadcasting Unit with a view to broadcasting on a programme called 'For Your Approval' - and no-one had bothered to tell me!!! I was, to put it mildly, furious, and cursed them up hill and down dale. Off I went to see Captain Hamer to see if I could borrow my jeep to go into Jerusalem and join them. Permission given I roared off into the wilderness, mad as a hatter, and caught up with them just as they were going into the sandbagged, barbed wired and heavily guarded Radio Station. They all had passes to gain entrance except me! I argued with the sentry that as I was one of the Concert Party; and they could do no less than back me up; the radio station had issued one pass too few and I should be allowed in. Weight of numbers and common sense prevailed and I was allowed in.

The sequel was poetic justice! C.S.M. Jack Pomeroy with his accordion and myself were first to broadcast. The audition was on January 5th and on Sunday January 6th we had a call from JCPA telling us we would broadcast on Wednesday 16th. I was ecstatic. My diary records "Gone mad with delight." On the Saturday I had made two small records with a message and a snatch of song and sent them to my mam and my wife.

Several members of the club managed to distinguish themselves on Radio Station JCPA in the program 'For Your Approval' which went out live at 18:15 hours on Wednesdays.

16th January 1946

Accordion	SQMS Jack Pomeroy (CC Admin Office Div. HQ)
Tenor	Sig. Ted Hold (Div. HQ Sigs)

30th January

Spanish Guitar	Pte. Frank Coulman (Div. HQ)
Hawaiian Guitar	Pte. Jack Thompson (Div. Sigs.)
Impersonator/String Bass	Driver Val De Rosa (74 Field Hygiene Sect)

4th February

Pianist	Sig. Smith (Div. HQ Sigs.)

Shows were also given at Sarafand College on 14th January 1946 and for 9th Para. Battalion on 19th January. It was en route to the latter that Reg Goodricke was injured in a smash! Later Pte. Stephenson left the Division, the producer sprained his ankle and Pte. Barrow RACC came in for a lot of hard work as associate producer and secretary!

I am not sure when we started to call ourselves 'The Jaacovians' and the show 'Crazy Antics' but it must have been very early on as an article in the 'Palestine Post', dated 15th February 1946, had this to say.

"Crazy Antics in the Ark"

"The Jaacovians, consisting of members of the 6th AB Div. Paid a return visit to the Services Club, Tel Aviv, in their show 'Crazy Antics'. As on the occasion of their first visit they played to a packed house and provided two hours of bright entertainment, the standard of some of the turns being such as would have done credit to a professional stage.

A number of the players including Sig. Smith, a very competent pianist, and CSM Jack Pomeroy, who plays the accordion for which he writes most of his own music, have recently broadcast from Jerusalem. During the course of the evening we saw Shakespeare as we have never seen it before; the Romeo of Cpl. Rogers being only equalled by the unorthodox Juliet provided by Pte. Chambers; these two members of the cast being responsible for most of the comedy during the evening. Pte. de Rosa gave some exceedingly effective impersonations, whilst Ted Hold proved a pleasing tenor.

The monologues dealt with historical events given by Cpl. Blackledge were never taught at school and were infinitely more amusing. Sig. Goodricke introduced some typical cockney humour and Pte. Ken Barrow, and his ukulele, provided a bright ten minutes. Sig. Thompson and Ptes. Coulman and de Rosa, billed as 'The Pegasus Trio', were musical as well as amusing and completed a thoroughly enjoyable evening.

In addition to producing the show and acting as an admirable compere, Sig. Dick Le Jeune appeared in a sketch in which he was adequately supported by Dvr. Moss and Sig. Hold."

#29   The cast of 'Crazy Antics' with Roger Livesey and Ursula Jeans

Back row: Reg Goodricke, "Chunky" Chambers, "Smudger" Smith, "Pablo" de Rosa, Dick Le Jeune, Lt. Barker. Front row: Jack Pomroy, Jock Duncan, Frank Coulman, Ken Barrow, Ursula Jeans, Roger Livesey, Ted Hold, "Red" Huish

I suppose we adopted the name 'The Jaacovians' from the village of Bir Jaacov near to our camp. A great bunch of lads and many happy memories. The outstanding memory for me however, apart from the broadcast, was whilst on the way back from a show in Amman, Trans-Jordan, on Monday 18th March 1946. We had stopped off for a swim in the Dead Sea and who should be there but Roger Livesey, and his wife Ursula Jeans, having a day off whilst on a tour in the Middle East. Of course we made the most of the occasion and they were both very kind to us.

In fact it was Roger Livesey who, when I sought his advice, suggested that as I was married and had a good job to go back to (demob was looming) not to aspire to the professional stage as so very few made it to the top. At the same time he was kind enough to say, "Carry on singing and enjoy your music."

Although I did not make it professionally I am still around and since 1946 have taken tenor lead in many musical comedies, operettas, G & S, and hundreds of concerts as an amateur and was once heard on Tyne Tees Television. I even managed to successfully produce a few shows before retiring from the stage. Even today I am still kept busy entertaining at social and other festive occasions and long may it continue, say I!

One last thought. I wonder if our Dick Le Jeune became Richard Lejeune BBC Producer? I have a faded, but cherished, programme from one of our shows which most of the cast signed on my demob (Oh Happy Day!). It cost 10 mils at the time but you couldn't buy it today at any price. I'll just rattle off the names of the performers - Dick Le Jeune, 'Red' Huish, Bill 'Smudger' Smith, 'Pablo' De Rosa, 'Pop' Rogers, 'Chunky' Chambers, Jack Pomeroy, 'Jock' Duncan, Frank Coulman, Ricky Jones, Reg Goodricke, Ken Barrow and yours truly, Ted Hold, that 'pleasing tenor'. As the waiters in 'The Ark Club' used to say, "Truly Allah! These Airborne wallahs are mad!"

If any reader is reminded of 'It Ain't Half Hot Mum' I will forgive him – but watch it! Most of us are veterans of Normandy, The Ardennes and The Rhine!

Chapter 17   The Perils of Palestine

The Div. were getting a 'bad press' in Palestine caused no doubt by the propaganda from the Hagannah, Stern Gang and Irgun Zvei Leumi. I hadn't realised how bad until one day when Peter Pitt - a recent addition via Tank Corps - and I were browsing through a wonderful bookshop in Jerusalem. We realised we were being closely observed by the two very attractive and beautifully 'bosomed' assistants. Eventually they plucked up courage enough to approach us and ask if they could help. Friendly conversation ensued during the course of which they rather timidly asked if we were members of the Sixth Airborne Div. On being assured that we were they looked puzzled and then puzzled us in turn by saying, "But you are gentlemen." Laughingly we assured them that this was so and asked why were they so surprised. It transpired that the local press had informed their readers that the Sixth A/B Div. consisted of criminals, murderers and jailbirds and were no better than the Gestapo.

It was probably due to this and the various 'incidents' taking place in Palestine and reported back in England that a P.R. exercise was mounted by the authorities to assure families back home that we were O.K. Part of this exercise took the form of 'interviews' with various members of the Div. and subsequent articles in their local press. I was interviewed by a Cpl. Morrice P.R.O. on January 4th and a small article subsequently appeared in the Sunderland Echo. But I must confess to over enthusiasm - the wings of my glider on landing in Normandy on D-Day were not "torn off" but they were damaged by 'Rommel's asparagus'.

But to get back to the gorgeous girls in the bookshop. We were invited to go home with them to meet their families and have tea. Tempting though the offer was we said we'd have to see what time we could get away from camp and would contact them at a later date. After due consideration we decided that as the Jews were making life generally miserable for us and would do anything, even murder, to get their hands on weapons and uniforms, discretion was the best bet and we never took those two very attractive girls up on their offer - we'll never know! We'd arrived in Palestine in September and on the 20th October Sarafand Camp was raided. On 31st October Lydda Railway Junction and Haifa Oil refinery were attacked and 240 other different locations were sabotaged. On November 14th there were riots in Jerusalem and Tel Aviv.

On December 26th I had parked my jeep in a car park in Jerusalem and started to walk up the road to hear a performance of 'The Messiah' at the Concert Hall, next to the NAFFI and opposite the King David Hotel. On my right was the Palestinian Police Station, barb wired, sand bagged and guarded. I walked past it and I was about half way up the hill when with one TREMENDOUS bang up went the Police Station and all hell broke loose. As I was unarmed and therefore not much use I carried on up the hill and into the NAFFI, a palatial building, to grab a cup of tea and a sandwich prior to the concert. It was deserted, not a soul in sight! For a moment I couldn't understand it then the penny dropped, they'd all taken shelter. Still wanting a cuppa I went on the prowl and eventually found one very frightened olive skinned gentleman hiding under a counter. He took quite a bit of persuading to come out of hiding but I eventually got what I came for.

The idea of listening to a performance of 'The Messiah' at Christmas time in Jerusalem had appealed to me tremendously and it was with eager anticipation that I settled down to the performance after my cuppa. With the exception of the tenor who I thought was a bit 'reedy' I enjoyed it very much but found its message of peace and hope and the beauty of the music very much at odds with the situation outside. It reminded me very much of the time in

Normandy when I had to return to the dangers of war after the peace and tranquility of 'The Song Of Bernadette'.

Bir Jaccov must have been close to Sarafand Camp because it was to the Sarafand Cinema that I went very frequently and saw some pretty good films, I also saw some that weren't. Outside the cinema were those ubiquitous vendors selling just about everything. Favourite among which was ice cold, freshly squeezed orange or grapefruit juice, quite delicious and irresistible. There were also mountains of roasted and salted monkey nuts, still in their shells, which were also delicious and irresistible. So much so in fact that I don't remember ever once going to the cinema when the floor was free of a thick carpet of monkey nut shells. Sweets, chocolate and ice cream were also available. There was also a small cafe, the Victoria Cafe, just outside the camp gates where we used to go for 'supper' usually consisting of a mixed grill washed down with half pints of port and lemon!!!

New Year's Eve 1945 and I'm on guard! The night is cold, the stars are brilliant and with the exception of the red glaring eyes, or were they green?, of the pi-dogs on the other side of the fence illuminated at intervals by the 'search light' I am all alone in the world. I am also feeling very unhappy. What the hell am I doing in this God-forsaken spot on New Year's Eve? I felt very bitter. Midnight arrived and in the distance real searchlights, reminiscent of air raids, performed a silent pirouette and with tears of frustration in my eyes I yelled, "Happy Effing New Year." Reply came there none! Welcome 1946!!! The strain was beginning to tell although I was not yet aware of it.

There were so many things going on at this time it is difficult to know how to put them all together. Perhaps likening it all to an ever-changing colourful, sometimes exciting and always interesting kaleidoscope would be just about right.

One ongoing interest was chess! Derek Hogarth, a very good and keen player, took me under his wing and taught me how to play. He had a lot of enjoyment systematically annihilating me time after time until one day I, to his utter amazement, and my own – beat him. My diary tells me it was on Friday February 8th 1946. Try as I might I never did it again.

In our spare time we played football, soft-ball, and basket-ball. Inter Section and Inter Unit competitions were held. I managed to score a goal in a game we lost and hit a home run in a game we won. We started a Section News magazine called 'How-Now', being 'H' Section. I instigated a page called 'Hackneyed Heraldry' which consisted of a facetious coat of arms, hand coloured, taking the mickey out of various people. One I remember was in reference to Captain Hamer who was a keen member of the Officers' Kennel Club and had at that time a plaster cast on his leg. Crossed bones and crutches and Pluto featured on the shield and the motto was 'Pro Bono Publico'. All my own work and all very well received.

#30   The H Section football team in October 1945

Back row: Grant, Busby, McMurram, Frame, Parker, Love

Front row: Ted Hold, Atkins, Struther, Cross, Creek

Most of the officers had acquired dogs of various shapes, sizes and breeds, probably as much as pets as guard dogs and one very funny incident resulted. One of the lads came in one day with the news that one of the officers had gone round the bend. He swore blind that this officer was standing on top of a small hill in the scrub shouting for a taxi! On investigation we found he was absolutely right, the officer was shouting for a taxi. It just so happened that 'Taxi' was the name of his dog! The chance was too good to miss so we all started shouting for a taxi! - until Taxi's boss's rank put a stop to the fun. A sense of humour did help to keep us sane. Sadly the Kennel Club didn't last long and sadder still neither did the dogs. Rabies, picked up no doubt from the pi-dogs, broke out among the pack and they had to be destroyed.

Guard duty and cookhouse fatigues were an on going activity whatever else may be happening and I came in for my share. Somewhere is a photograph of me wearing a sack apron and up to my arms in greasy pans - and I'm laughing!!!

Nobody was laughing one day when we found the bread liberally studded with weevils. Any complaints? Most certainly there were.

 # 31   Ted seeing the funny side of fatigues in December 1945

"Right", said the Duty Officer, "Tomorrow I will collect samples, have them ready on the end of each table."

We were messing in marquees at the time and the tables, end to end, were the length of the marquee. Next morning a mountain of bread wrapped weevils awaited him on each table. They were duly and solemnly collected. A parade was held the next morning when the O.C. said,

"With regard to the complaints about weevils in the bread. I have asked the Senior Medical Officer to have a word with you" - The Senior Medical Officer! In effect what the S.M.O. said amounted to - not only would the weevils do us no harm but they were in fact highly nutritious! A case of HERE no weevil SEE no weevil SPEAK no weevil! This happened during a period when none of the food was particularly palatable, so much so in fact that the swill-bins (empty oil drums) did a roaring trade. A sickening sight ensued of Arab kids diving into the bins, legs waving in the air, filling tins with slops to take away and eat.

Once we'd moved to Bir Jaccov we of course lost the Med! No more cooling off and cavorting in the sea. Somebody however discovered that the Veterinary Corps in the Arab town of Ramle had a swimming pool and once in a while we would be given permission by the Vet. Corps to have a dip. The pool was on, or should that be in, the top of a rectangular building with a typical Middle East dome on pillars making an open sided roof. Access was by steps from a courtyard. The pool was about 12 feet square by 12 feet deep and absolute heaven. The dimensions of the pool limited the number of bodies at any one time but we managed very well.

It was at Ramle, en route somewhere with the 'Crazy Antics', that I witnessed a bizarre spectacle. Each house and adjoining house had a flat roof which stood a couple of feet or so higher than its neighbours and there, running for his life across the roof tops, was a young boy. In hot pursuit was a 'rampant' native who, as the young lad was climbing onto each successive roof, helped him up with a thrust of his buttocks. In the street stood a large appreciative crowd cheering them on. It wasn't long before we joined in cheering. The lorry inevitably moved on and we were left wondering was it just good-natured fun or for real?

Round the next corner was for real, a stinking open tannery and the smell was appalling! Next door was a school with an open scrub playground into which the kids came scrambling, 'play-time' no doubt. I don't know if proper toilet facilities were available, probably not, as the kids just 'up with their nighties' and relieved themselves anywhere. Hygiene in Ramle, as in the rest of the Arab populated area of Palestine, seemed to be in very short supply.

The abiding memory I have of the Arab/Palestinian population is one of an indolent; except when it came to thieving; 'Allah will provide' bunch still living in Biblical times and some of them an evil looking lot. They did have radios and cars but no highway code, no traffic lights or road signs and 'the devil take the hindmost'. Each 'hole in the wall' shop, cafe or whatever had its own 'blaster' and not all tuned in to the same station. The local music has to be heard to be believed, and the singing is akin to the high and low pitched moans, groans, sobs and ululating shrieks you could reasonably expect to hear from some poor, constipated, tortured soul trying to relieve themselves through a painfully pilitic orifice! Soul music indeed!

Thinking of local driving! There was an occasion when I was to drive a Corporal Adams and Captain Hamer from Bir Jaccov to Ramle. The Captain had business to transact and Corporal Adams was going home - demobbed - via Ramle railway station. With a train to catch we were moving along quite happily when we were slowed down by a lorry which from the rear resembled a mobile haystack. The driving cab was just not visible. On the right is an embankment with no turnings, on the left a road length ditch and miles of open fields! Captain Hamer got very frustrated and ordered me to get past him. There wasn't a lot of room to get past even though we were the only two vehicles on the road so I gave him a few blasts on the horn and eventually he slowed down and moved over to the right! I pulled over to the left and put my foot down. I was just catching him up when the bastard turned sharp left to head over a culvert and down a track into the field. No signs, no signals, no warning! A crash was inevitable as I must have been doing at least 50 m.p.h. I did three things, braked, changed into 1st gear and swung the wheels to go with the lorry to the left. Hamer was also hanging on the steering wheel and pulling it round.

First gear and brakes helped enormously but I must have been doing at least 10 to 15 m.p.h. when I hit the parapet of the culvert and came to a sudden and jarring halt. Hamer shot out of the jeep and pulled the driver out of his cab and started to bollick him good and proper. Corporal Adams shot out of the jeep and came round to me and I honestly thought he was going to hit me for nearly getting him killed. On the contrary, he grabbed my hand and pumped it up and down and thanked me for marvellous driving and added, "I don't know how the hell you missed him, I don't know how the hell you stopped!" I don't think I did either! Anyhow he was very happy to not get killed on his way home for demob and kept telling me so. Captain

Hamer couldn't get any sense out of the lorry driver so he took a description of the vehicle and its engine number.

#32   Ted and 'NANKI-POO' at Nuseirat in November 1945

We duly and carefully got to Ramle, Corporal Adams thanked me again and said goodbye. Captain Hamer went about his business and my jeep went into REME workshops to check on any damage - we could have had a cracked chassis! All, however, was well and I have no recollection of the return journey. My diary tells me it all happened on 9th March. It also tells me I went to see 'Madonna of the Seven Moons' in Sarafand that night, which was a Saturday, and reads, "Thank God I am alive and no one was hurt in the accident."

Early on I had christened my jeep 'Nanki-Poo' and painted the name on the front. I suppose it was because ever since being in the chorus of 'The Mikado' in Salisbury I'd had an ambition to play the role. To such an extent in fact that I felt like identifying with the character. I was to achieve that ambition in 1958 with a local amateur operatic group. We all did our own maintenance and I looked after 'Nanki-Poo' very well keeping it up to scratch and immaculate. It was my third jeep during my service with the 6th A/B Div. and it served me well, to such an extent in fact that once behind the wheel it became an extension of myself and I was in full control and it did all I asked of it. On one particular occasion I was to be very glad of that.

One afternoon I had to go from Gaza to Sarafand, or to Ramle, to pick up a new trailer accompanied by a Corporal Benyon. It was a long journey and on the way out we found ourselves being tailed by a pack of pi-dogs who seemed somewhat more than interested in our presence. Not wishing to be savaged by a pack of rabid dogs I put my foot down and left them behind in a trail of billowing dust.

By the time we had collected the trailer, had a bite to eat and set out on the return journey the sun was very low on the hilltops and before we got halfway 'home' it was dark. Not a soul or another vehicle was in sight for miles until, coming through a valley, we could see in the distance tracer going from left to right across the road. I stopped and switched off the headlights and watched. We pondered on the possibility of it being a night exercise using real ammo but when the tracer fire was apparently returned we decided it was an ambush of some sort. What to do? We had no weapons and we couldn't stop there all night and we didn't know which side of the road was ours so I said to Benyon, "Get your head down and hang on, we're going through", and I let 'Nanki-Poo' off the leash.

I was vaguely aware of a figure trying to wave us down as we tore along the road, still without headlights, at about 60 m.p.h. I was however not going to stop to ask' "Are you a terrorist or a Para, or a terrorist in a Para uniform?", and went through driving appropriately enough like 'JEHU'. A minute later, my foot still hard down, the road turned sharp left over a little low parapet bridge across a wadi and then sharp right to continue in the direction we had originally been travelling. Whipping left and then right I got through the 'chicane' without turning over even though the empty trailer was twice airborne and threatening to part company with the jeep. Much later on Benyon had a great time recounting the tale to anyone who would listen and I can still hear him saying, "And you should have seen this bugger drive."

During my Palestine sojourn I had the good fortune to visit Jerusalem, Bethlehem and the Mount of Olives, also Tel Aviv and Gaza of Samson fame, and found them all fascinating. I also passed through Amman, the then capital of Trans-Jordan, and it was fascinating to see the Roman amphitheatre just off the roadside. In Jerusalem I went through St Stephen's Gate and via the Via Dolorosa to the church of the Holy Sepulchre and found it difficult to understand why the site of the Crucifixion, the site of the nailing to the cross, and the site of the Holy Sepulchre should all be under one roof! Not only that, there was really nothing to see except marble slabs, altars, chapels, lamps, icons and statuettes adorned with a myriad jewels. Gilding the Lily bore no comparison.

"There is a green hill far away"? Not any more there ain't, not for nearly two thousand years! That is always presupposing it was green in the first place, which I doubt! Constantine and Theodora must take a lot of the blame for that and more of the blame for a vast amount of 'evidence' disappearing during the Nicean amalgamation and sieving of the Christian Sects extant at that time. I could appreciate the overturning of the moneylenders' tables in the Temple and I wanted to kick a few backsides myself as the traders tried to follow us into the church still peddling their wares. The 'Sects' I found were still with us.

One visit with the Padre to the church of the Holy Sepulchre coincided with the Feast of Pentecost when 'God sent fire from Heaven'. All the local sects, tribes, villages etc. had gathered in and around the Church. Not only was it packed inside, and in the courtyard outside, but every roof top was precariously crowded. They were all carrying candles or tapers and were waiting for the moment when the Archimandrite (Greek Orthodox priest) enters the Holy Sepulchre and 'God' ignites a flame which the priest puts forth through purpose built holes in the wall of the chapel of the Sepulchre and they all surge forward to be the first to light their own candle. The light is transmitted from one to the other and they all want to be first.

Every sect, tribe, village and individual wants to be first. In the most 'Holy of Holies' tempers frayed, fighting ensued, knives flashed and all hell broke out. On that particular pilgrimage two ambulances took away the injured and I did hear there were also two or three killed.

Bethlehem was like the Garden of Eden by comparison, en route to which, Bethlehem - not the Garden of Eden, we stopped by the roadside to look at the Roman aqueduct which had brought water to Jerusalem. Just a pipeline, broken and exposed, but authentic. We also had a look at Rachel's tomb which purports to be authentic but? You could also take your pick of any one of half a dozen 'fields'; scrubland really; in which the "shepherds watched their flocks by night." It all depended on whom you were daft enough to ask, "Do you know which field it was where the shepherds watched their flocks?"

The town of Bethlehem was small and commercial. Shops abounded, all selling the usual 'Holy' paraphernalia and Middle East specialities, silver, brass and leather ware, silks, brocades etc. I bought a 'made on the premises', mother of pearl brooch and earrings and a 'silver' compact which I had suitably inscribed for my wife Ena and I'm glad to say she still has it. The traders of course followed us right to the door of the Church of the Nativity and we had to forcibly stop them from following us inside. The entrance door is very low and small, and was made so to prevent the Crusaders riding in on horse back - or so I read somewhere. There was however, no doubt about the Crusaders' crosses hacked into the church pillars. Very historic and romantic. Once again of course lamps, gleaming brass icons and candles proliferated and the 'site' of the birth of Jesus, the Stable and Manger, was all marble, walls, ceiling and floor, and in a niche was a large golden star inlaid in the floor. Strangely enough there was an all pervading sense of peacefulness but I suppose it all depended on the mental attitude with which you approached the spot. Even so I felt a great sense of peace. I liked Bethlehem.

Another place I liked was the Garden of Gethsemane which is on the other side of the valley of Kidron opposite the Golden Gate (bricked up) in the city wall of Jerusalem. The site of the garden is quite high and a wonderful view of old Jerusalem and the city wall is to be had across the valley. The 'garden' is dotted with rocks, olive trees and pine trees and is quite green and apart from the inevitable church I found I could mentally associate what I was looking at with the Biblical story. The trees of course couldn't be 2000 years old but I felt that the 'untouched by human hand' natural scenery in Palestine, the hills and valleys and the wilderness, couldn't have changed all that much and that, in that one respect at least, I was looking back in time.

January 22nd we moved to a training camp at El Faluja with HQRA. It was an unused new aerodrome with quite a large power room near the main gates. That, as I was informed by Captain Hamer, was now my responsibility and I was to provide power for the camp. The building housed two diesel generators one having a greater output than the other. They were in immaculate condition as was the rest of the power room and switch gear. The only problem was, I knew damn all about them! I didn't even know how to start them! I needn't have worried. Their immaculate condition was due to a Palestinian - Ishmael - who was the caretaker and knew everything I needed to know and between us we gave the camp all the power they needed! He was a gentleman and we got on well together until I inadvertently upset the applecart.

He got into the habit of bringing me a chappati every day and I felt obliged to accept his hospitality and eat them, tasteless as they were, and each one with several sets of fingerprints visible. After a day or two I'd had more than enough of chappatis and after a token bite or two managed, unknown to him, to hide the remains in a culvert which ran underneath the pathway leading across a storm drain around the power house. As a token of my appreciation I felt obliged to return his hospitality by sharing some of my food with him.

All went well until one day when I came back from wherever I'd been and he confronted me in a very wild and agitated state. Someone had told him that I'd fed him pork, which was taboo in his religion, and he was very upset. It had never occurred to me that Spam sandwiches could cause so much trouble and I lied like hell in telling him I hadn't given him pork. I don't think he was convinced for he went outside, stuck his fingers down his throat and heaved his inside up. For the next day or so I had the distinct feeling that he looked on me with a jaundiced eye. I, on my part, behaved as if all was normal.

On the 24th January there was a terrible accident on the firing range. A 4.2 mortar bomb exploded prematurely killing six and wounding two of the R.A. personnel.

Apart from my job in the powerhouse I was still performing my usual duties and my diary informs me that I repaired three 'welfare' sets and took Ishmael's photo. Ishmael had a cousin Ahmed who had black teeth and stinking breath who was often around and had taken quite a strong liking to me - God knows why! I got really worried about it the next day however when I had to leave the camp and take Sgt. Price to Ramle - Ahmed wept to see me go!!! I felt like Lawrence of Arabia! I was very tired on my return and retired early.

Next day after duty I went to Tel Aviv in the evening to do a concert with 'Crazy Antics' returning at 12:30 a.m. The next three days I was ill and barely able to do my duty and on the 30th and 31st of January and 1st of February it rained and rained and washed all the chappatis out of the culvert. On February 5th I said goodbye and thank you to Ishmael and Ahmed and damn me if he didn't weep huge crocodile tears again.

 # 33   Ahmed, Ted and Ishmael outside the El Faluja power plant in February 1946

Chapter 18 Homeward Bound

Physically I wasn't in good shape around now and I was fretting to be home. I was beginning to creak and I think I was on the verge of a breakdown. The news of my granda's death on the 6th of March didn't help. I threw myself into helping out in the church (two marquees), gathering palms and flowers for decoration, attending services and leading the hymn singing, usually I pitched the hymns too high. I also got involved in an Education Scheme doing lectures on Magnetism, Electricity and Radio - well it carried Sergeant's stripes but it amounted to nothing. Then the Army decided to reassess everyone and have a Trades Test! Practical work I could do but theory after all this time? It didn't help my mental state, which in turn didn't help my health. I'd had it, I wanted out!!! As things turned out I didn't do badly in the Test but neither did I do well.

April 6th 1946. My 25th birthday and I'm on a 24 hour guard duty. Happy Birthday Ted!!!

April 13th and 14th. Terrific cold, headache, toothache, sore throat but soldiered on, even going to Church both days.

April 15th. Brought yet another trial, 'Crazy Antics' decided to audition and reassess everyone. I don't think I ever knew the result and I don't even remember the event except as a diary note.

By the 16th I was feeling a bit better and on the 19th, Good Friday, as I was going from 'A to B' in the camp during the afternoon I passed Padre Hall who said "Oh! Ted, your 'B release' has come through!!!" At first I couldn't believe it but he assured me it was true and suddenly the clouds lifted, the sun shone, there was a rainbow in the sky, bells were ringing and I'd never felt better in my whole life. I was going home at last. I was so moved I hardly heard him inviting me to accompany him to Jerusalem.

We went the following day, Saturday 20th April 1946, to the Church of the Holy Sepulchre. It was my second visit. The first time was on November 30th 1945 as a pilgrim and I was given (I actually paid) a tiny splinter of rock about as big as a half a pin encased in candle-grease which was supposed to be from the site of the Crucifixion. I also received a Certificate of Pilgrimage signed by the Archimandrite Kyrin(?), Guardian of the Church of the Holy Sepulchre. I still have it but the splinter of Golgotha I'm afraid has not survived. Now I'm on my second visit, as an act of thanksgiving, I suppose, for my survival and for my release and only those who have enjoyed the same experience will know how I felt.

One final memory before I set off on my way home. Round about the end of January and the beginning of February when I was really ill and actually 'lost' a day out of the five or so days, during which I'm sure I must have spent some time unconscious, oddly enough, no one seemed to know and I was too ill to care! No one came looking for me, no guards, no fatigues, no duties of any sort, no nothing. I was lost in a fog. It was very strange. Only one incident which occurred during this time, and the only one I can remember, I remember vividly. I am lying on my bed, in the corner of the stores tent, with my arm dangling over the edge, fingers two or three inches above the sand and I am sound asleep. I was awakened by a slight tickling sensation in my fingertips. Very slowly and very carefully and without moving my hand I gently looked over the edge of the bed. There on the sand and standing erect was a very small and very beautiful golden coloured mouse sniffing my fingers and tickling them with its whiskers. I was, to say the least, entranced and watched it for quite a while and until, having decided I was too big to eat, it moved under my bed, out of sight and out of my life. Feeling at peace with the world I turned over and slept like a child. I'd just had a visitor!

After the trip to Jerusalem with the Padre I spent the next few days saying my goodbyes to the lads in H Section, the Concert Party and anyone else who cared. I also spent a lot of time checking and returning tools and equipment in my charge. All went well until it came to handing over the jeep, 'Nanki-Poo'! There was one tool missing - a screwdriver!!! The fact that the Section Officer had been running all over Palestine for the last six weeks or so with my jeep cut no ice! I'd signed for it - I was responsible - I was on a charge!!! I was duly hauled before the C.O. and charged. I should have been double charged as I had to pay for the tool that I had lost and also pay for a replacement. I didn't argue, I wanted out!

The following day I'm one of about ten blokes who are on parade in front of the C.O. who gave us a pep talk on being good lads when we got home and don't let the side down. He thanked us collectively for our service and then came down the line shaking hands with everyone. I was on the end of the row and as he shook hands with me he looked slightly puzzled and said, "Haven't I seen you somewhere before?"

"Yes sir", I said with a broad grin, "You had me on a charge for losing a screwdriver, yesterday"

"Ah! yes", he said and I saw him grin as he turned away.

25th April and the train left Quastina for Asluj where we stayed the night. The next day we crossed the Sinai and the Suez Canal to the West Bank and stayed the night.

27th April we left the railway station at El Quassassin and arrived at Alexandria where we were transported to a transit camp at Sidi Bishr. En route to which I remember seeing hundreds of Arabs in long white Jellabies marching through the streets, waving banners and yelling their heads off! It didn't look like a welcoming committee. It is also possible that is why we were behind barbed wire fences for the next few days until a ship was available. If we'd got out among that lot I hate to think what might have happened.

The monotony of that long train journey was relieved by the vendors who besieged us every time we stopped. On sale were watches, bags, carpets, drinks, sweets, nuts, fruit, silks and a myriad trinkets.

I remember one of our lads standing by the door haggling with a local over the price of a watch. The train started to move and the vendor jumped aboard trying to get paid or his watch back. He got neither, instead he got a boot in the belly and was pushed off the train. Another got on the train carrying a tray slung from his neck in which were forty or so compartments filled with multi-coloured nuts and sweetmeats - reminded me of the choc. and ice cream girls of my youthful cinema days. Down the middle of the coach he wandered, seats on either side, trying to sell his wares. The fun started when someone on his left attracted his attention whilst someone on his right helped himself from that side of the tray. Then the position would be reversed. When he twigged what was happening he set off at a little faster pace trying to get out of our coach. He was doing alright until someone stuck his foot out - the floor became a multi-coloured carpet!

It wasn't all one sided however. One of the items we had been allowed to take with us was a blanket. Well it did get cold at night. During the day however it was sweltering and every door and window was wide open to catch whatever little breeze we could. Some of the time we spent looking out of the windows at the stark silhouette of the train in the sand as we steamed along but most of the time we dozed. One of the lads, in a corner seat, had his blanket rolled up and was using it as a pillow behind his head. Suddenly a brown arm came, from the roof, through the window and whipped his blanket away. He was rudely awakened as his head hit the woodwork and he let out a yell which woke everyone else up. "Some bugger's pinched me blanket", he yelled, pointing to the window. There, to the roof of our silhouette train was now added the black silhouette of a figure waving a blanket - and it was running. In a flash some of the lads were up on the roof and a chase ensued which we watched - in silhouette. It was just like an old silent Mack Sennett film - hilarious! The end of the tale is that the thief jumped off the roof onto the sand and stood grinning at us and dancing up and down waving the blanket as we steamed off across the desert. He wasn't lost and he knew we wouldn't follow him - or we'd be lost.

Four fretful days followed when we got to Sidi Bishr but at long last on the 20th May we were wakened at 5 a.m. to board the troop ship 'Staffordshire' at 9 a.m. We sailed at 5:30 p.m. en route for Toulon. Once again we were in hammocks and my diary says – "horrible!" Honestly, I don't remember! The route we were to follow was known as 'Medlock'.

3rd May and we were in the Med. and it was blowy. I was up at 4:30 a.m. and slept on deck.

4th Still in Med. and calm and brilliant.

5th 8 a.m. and here we are between Italy and Sicily. Messina Straits at 11 a.m. and a great view of Stromboli.

That night we had a ship's concert in the First Class Lounge. I remember the 'compere' who introduced a flautist as "The Fluter-rer-rer"!, I kid you not, also Alan Chape, who I was to meet later in Fellowship, telling some crude stories. One in particular about an Italian band, Mussolini and Hitler wasn't too bad but the 'farting contest' was to put it mildly - ripe!

6th and we're heading for Sardinia and Corsica and another concert this time on C Deck. Same as before including 'the Fluter-rer-rer'.

The odd thing about the concerts was that we didn't have a piano and I couldn't help thinking was this due to the Aussies? Apparently on a previous voyage a bunch of Australians had wanted to use the piano for a sing-song but were told they couldn't have the key, it wasn't allowed. The result of that was – one piano on the bottom of the Med!

7th 7 a.m. and we've arrived at Toulon via the Bonifaccio Straights, Sardinia and Corsica. It was a strange feeling sailing past the scuppered French Fleet at Toulon and seeing the wreckage, especially the upper decks and masts of the 'Richelieu' - a sad sight really. We landed at Toulon between 8 a.m. and 9 a.m. On the 8th we arrived at a place called Bram, or Brum, for breakfast - Oh! I'm on a train from Toulon. We went through Paris about 4 a.m.

The 9th saw us at Boulogne en route for Calais arriving at 7.50 a.m. At 12 noon we crossed the Channel for Dover - a wonderful sight - arriving at 1.30 p.m. I sent a postcard to Ena. Saw a film 'Dolly's Sisters' and had some fish and chips - sounds like a night on the town!

On the following day the 10th, I left Dover Priory at 8.30 a.m., phoned Ena from York, got to Thirsk at about 5 p.m. and finished up at Knayton Camp. I slept badly.

On the 11th we found ourselves employed shovelling coal and coke from one bunker to another. It was the Army's way of keeping us occupied and out of trouble. I found it degrading and demeaning for veterans to have to suffer this sort of treatment at the end of nearly four years of faithful and meritorious service and I said so.

"I'm in charge", said the N.C.O., "and you do as I say or you don't get home" - we did! The next day brought more degradation. Shovelling at a higher level though, for the Officers Mess. We also de-kitted - gave them back our bits and pieces.

On the 13th I rang Ena and went to York to collect demob civvies. A suit, a trilby, vest, pants, shirt, shoes and socks. Then it was back to Knayton for cigarettes and various documents, discharge papers and especially coupons as most things were still on ration. I remember we were told we would be approached to sell our clothes but on no account to do it as we wouldn't have the coupons to get more.

I left Thirsk at 7.04 for home and I've no idea when I got to Sunderland but at least I was out of the Army and I was home for good. My war was over.

Chapter 19   We'll Meet Again

The Belgians

Before leaving Neffe in 1945 I promised Camille, Emma and Nelly that I would keep in touch, which I duly did. In 1954 received a wonderful invitation to have a holiday with them at the Chateau - courtesy of the Prince and Princess de Merode of course; albeit dining below stairs and sleeping in the servants quarters.

Ena and I and our son Anthony, who was four, had a wonderful time but only one story is really relevant.

Pierre, who I think was a cousin of Camille, was the local barber in the village of St Gerard, or maybe it was Bioul. And like most barbers he was a lively, witty and garrulous person. One day Camille took us to have dinner and tea with him. Pierre's shop was in the middle of one side of an open rectangle of houses, the opposite end being open and void of buildings. As Ena, Anthony and I walked down the street towards the barber's shop quite a few people came to their doorways to bid us "Bonjour Monsieur, Madame, comment ca vas?" and so on. Others peered from behind their curtains, all very friendly! Once inside Pierre's the atmosphere again was very friendly. Everybody wanted to see us and shake hands, the whole village seemed to need a haircut, the place was full. I remember being asked if I'd liked staying at the Chateau etc., etc. When it came time to leave we had a very friendly send-off. Everybody had been so kind.

Two or three days before this the newspapers carried a story that Gen. Bols, Divisional Commander of the 6th A/B during the war, was returning to the Ardennes and was to be a guest of Prince Frederic de Merode at the Chateau de Neffe. The General, who spoke French, was to be accompanied by his wife, who spoke just a little French, and their young son. The story had been the number one topic of conversation in Pierre's barber's shop for days and more so when Pierre informed everybody that the General and his wife and son were coming to dine with him! So there we were - famous for an afternoon, General Bols and family - and we didn't know. It's probably just as well - I might have spoiled it.

Camille and Pierre of course had set the hoax up and I was the unwitting pawn but I must confess to enjoying the thought even almost 50 years after.

I also enjoy the memory of my son Anthony playing hide and seek with the young Prince Alexandre de Merode in the huge kitchen of the Chateau and can still hear him calling "Prince, Prince" whilst searching for him. It was the same Prince Alexandre who became head of the International Red Cross Organisation.

While we said our farewells to Camille and Emma and the Chateau de Neffe we made our way to Brussels to meet Nelly. The young Princess Therese was at school in Brussels and of course Nelly was still 'nursemaid'. At that time Therese was living in Brussels and Nelly took us to visit her. Therese had a little friend with her, Jean, and I remember the train set and pet rabbits.

I think it was also the time I was 'granted an audience' with Princess Therese's grandmother, 'Marie Louise Isabelle, Caroline, Francoise de Paule, Laurence, Princess de Merode nee Princess de Bauffremont Courtenay'. She somehow or other knew about me and my friendship with 'the family' and had asked to meet me.

She was living in a suite at 8 Avenue Louise. I was taken there and having waited in a corridor for a while was then ushered into her presence. Literally 'ushered' by an attendant. It was like meeting Royalty and no wonder, I think she was related to the Belgian Royal Family or should that be the French Royal Family. We conversed for a short while about the holiday, the weather, my family and each other's health and then complimenting me on my French I was 'dismissed'. I felt as if I'd just met Queen Victoria - there was that aura about her. Sadly, she died in 1955, the following year, but I can always say I met her and I have an invitation to her funeral, but of course only as a souvenir.

From a schoolgirl in Brussels, Therese grew to be a beautiful lady who was an accomplished horsewoman and an expert huntswoman as well as excelling at blowing the hunting horn – winning many competitions. She also had her own stables in France and the South of England. She was also an excellent driver with a top class car. I almost forgot! She is now a tremendous motor-cyclist and goes roaring off all over the world on rallies and competitions.

 # 34   Nelly & Princess Thérèse   Princess Thérèse

We had regularly corresponded but the next time we met was when she brought Nelly to stay for a holiday with us. It was in 1968 and we were living in Grindon, Sunderland. She stayed for tea and then roared off in her sports car leaving Nelly with us for the next few days.

In 1976 Ena had to have her leg amputated and as soon as Therese heard the news a magnificent bunch of flowers arrived at the hospital. Once Ena was able to walk a little on her artificial limb, and I was adept at pushing her wheelchair, we got out and about and holidays were no great problem.

In the meantime many things had happened to Therese and few of them were good. She had her own stables at Melleroy south of Paris and quite a spread it was. Unfortunately whilst riding in Switzerland she had a bad fall and literally shattered the bones in her leg. A wonderful Swiss surgeon was able to put the jig-saw of bones together – her words – and save her leg but her competitive riding days were over. On top of that, pesticides spread in the fields by the farmers around Melleroy got into her horses feed and they were all poisoned.

This was the scenario when I got an invitation from her to spend a holiday at 'La Pichotterie', Melleroy, Chateaurenard. For a fortnight, July 16th – 30th 1990, Ena, Anthony and I enjoyed living like royalty visiting, among other places, Orleans, Blois, Cheverney, Chambord and Rogny Canal as well as having a wonderful, crazy railway trip on a track which had been severely buckled by the intense heat. The food, wine, hospitality, friendship and generosity were overwhelming. For the quiet moments there was the pond, home to flocks of wild ducks which had made a home from home. There were also the hens, rabbits, turkeys and the garden of vegetables. Just Heaven! Oh! And a crazy game of croquet on a field where the horses had been exercised – not exactly a lawn! I have never been able to adequately thank her and her friendship didn't stop there.

On 15th August 2000 Ena sadly died and Therese sent a wonderful bouquet. Then, on 6th April 2001, my family gave me a surprise 80th Birthday Party with a 'This Is Your Life' theme and once again a beautiful bouquet and personal note came from Therese.

She's one hell of a woman, kind, compassionate and generous and I'm a lucky man to be able to call her friend.

The Dutch

Many letters and Christmas greetings went back and forward from Sunderland to Panningen. Somehow I lost touch for a while but in 1978 thanks to two young Dutch girls visiting Sunderland I got in touch once more. The crowning moment came in 1985 on the 40th anniversary of Operation Varsity when, having told the Heuvelmann family of my plans, I took time off from the Pilgrimage and went to see them.

It was a joyous reunion with the Mother and her sister Maria, Mia and Ton her husband who was responsible for my transport to Panningen, Luke and Bernadette and family. Willy, who was by now a Catholic priest and Dean of Roermond was unable to be present but it was a very emotional reunion. Sadly, since then, the Mother, Maria, Willy and Ton have died.

I am still, however, in touch and courtesy of my Dutch friends in Wageningen, Bert and Cornelia de Boer, I have been able to visit Mia, Luke and Bernadette more than once in the last ten years.

And the Germans…

The Pilgrimage in March 1985, on the 40th anniversary of Operation Varsity, was the first return to the area of the Airborne drop in Germany for many Veterans, including myself. Now, proudly wearing our red berets and rows of medals, the 6th A/B Div. veterans sat in the coach en route for the cemetery in the Reichwald Forest, two and a half miles from Venlo, where so many of our comrades lay buried among the 7640 graves.

Crossing the Dutch / German border, as it was then, the coach was stopped by German guards who boarded and demanded, "Passports please, passports."

From the back of the coach came the reply, "You didn't ask for passports last time we came." A roar of approval, laughter and applause followed. The German guards looking decidedly uncomfortable did the only thing possible and got off the coach!

The End

POSTSCRIPT

When I received the following letter I thought that fate was giving me the chance to achieve my ambition of 1942.

ROCK LODGE

ROKER 28.10.53

Dear Sir,

Col L Laing the Sector Commander of the Sunderland Home Guard has asked me to get into touch with you with a view to you taking up the appointment of Signals Officer on his staff.

Will you please fill up the card enclosed and return it in the franked addressed envelope enclosed.

Would it be possible for you to see me at this Head Quarters I will then explain the present set up of the new Home Guard.

Thanking you B Stubbs. PDJ

I duly presented myself at ROCK LODGE, was interviewed and happily accepted. For two weeks I was very pleased with myself and then this letter arrived.

Tel: Sunderland 59465   9/15/G

Subject: - Home Guard

Mr E Hold,
5 Egerton Street
Hendon
SUNDERLAND

12 Nov 1953

Dear Mr Hold

I have this morning received a reply from your Records Office at Reading. They will not allow us to enrol you on the strength of this Unit.

Thank you for your kind offer of Service, I am very sorry they have turned it down.

B STUBBS H/Q

Apparently as a CLASS W Reservist, the Army still had me!

Enough to NOT give me the pip, wasn't it?